Automotive
FIBREGLASS
Fabrication and repair

Automotive
FIBREGLASS
Fabrication and repair

First published 2009
Copyright Performance Publishing Ltd

ISBN 978-0-9557418-2-1

Published by **Performance Publishing Ltd**
County House, 3 Shelley Road, Worthing, West Sussex BN11 1TT

Author:	John Dickens
Editor:	Ian Stent
Computer Graphics:	Grapevine Print & Marketing Ltd.
Page design:	James Mansell
Printing:	Grapevine Print & Marketing Ltd.

DISCLAIMER
Whilst every effort has been taken to ensure the accuracy of the information given in this book, no
liability can be accepted by the author, publisher or distributor for any loss, damage or injury
caused by errors in, omissions from, or misuse of the information given.

About the author

John Dickens was born in Leeds, Yorkshire and lived there for 20 years before obtaining a Chemistry degree at Teesside and a teaching qualification at Newcastle upon Tyne. He worked as a Chemistry teacher in the North-East of England for the next 35 years before retiring and becoming a technical writer for *Complete Kit Car* magazine.

From an early age John was involved with motor vehicles, initially with his father's motorcycles and cars then later with his own. He has built and owned a number of kit cars and motorcycles and also raced kit cars in the early years of the 750MC Kit Car Challenge. John regularly contributes technical articles to a number of owners' club publications and forums. He is married with two grown up sons and still lives in the Durham area.

Acknowledgements

Although I have written technical articles in the past, this is my first attempt at a complete book. As a result I am immensely grateful for the advice and encouragement of my editor Ian Stent during the whole process.

This book would definitely not have been completed without the help and understanding of my wife Toni. Not only did she spend hours in the garage taking most of the photos included in the book but she, and my son Paul, also lived with the smell of polyester resin permeating the whole house for long periods of time while the projects were being produced.

I am grateful to East Coast Fibreglass for allowing me free run of their premises to take photographs of their materials stock, Martin Cowell of bigHead Fasteners for providing samples of their products and also to MNR Sportscars who provided panels featured in the repairs section. Car owners Stefan Carlton, Simon Haydn, Richard Porter and Craig Smith provided photographs of gelcoat damage.

Contents

Introduction

I learned to work with GRP out of necessity rather than choice. My education began at an early age when my father swapped his motorcycle and sidecar *(Pic 1)* for a Reliant Regal, a GRP bodied 3-wheeled car.

Between us we quickly learned, after a fashion, how to use the small repair kits available from motor accessory shops to carry out minor body repairs although, looking back, the results were never more than adequate. I continued the family transport tradition with a Bond 875 and a Bond Bug (both GRP bodied 3-wheelers) before moving briefly onto a Mini, then back to GRP again with a series of kit cars which continues to the present day. Along the way, through enforced practice, I learned from my many mistakes and unsatisfactory results and gradually came to appreciate the full potential and versatility of glassfibre as a material and to become more skilled in its use. In recent years I produced a complete new front, wheel arches, sills and rear spoiler for my Mini Marcos racer *(Pic top and 2)* and a complete GRP body tub/chassis for my GTM Coupé *(Pic 3)*.

In writing this book my aim is to help others avoid the mistakes I made, whilst introducing them to the range of possibilities offered by GRP fabrication. If you have never used glassfibre or resin before you will find detailed instructions which take you step-by-step through the whole process. If you are already familiar with the small glassfibre kits available through motor accessory shops and have used them to carry out small bodywork or other repairs, this book will tell you how to get the best results with the least grief from these products. If you have reached the point where you are ready to try your hand at more ambitious projects such as component fabrication in GRP, you will find information on the range of products available, their suitability and

Me on my Dad's 500cc BSA B33

My modified Mini Marcos racer. This car was eventually purchased by Marcos Heritage and used as the prototype for their Mk VI GT kit.

limitations and detailed instructions on their use. This will enable you to select and use the ideal materials for your particular project. Being mindful of the fact that, like me, you are probably working in a standard single car garage or small workshop, I have also included advice on setting up a suitable working area and suggested some basic tools needed when working with the materials. The detailed instructions for using GRP are in the form of a series of projects. Starting with simple projects requiring only basic methods, each subsequent project demonstrates a new technique or the use of a new material. I have tried to make each project essentially self-contained. To avoid frequent and annoying cross reference between the chapters, some of the basic instructions will be repeated in each chapter.

Whenever practical instruction or advice is given it is based entirely on my own personal experience. I am not a trained GRP laminator and it may be that in some circumstances a professional would have a different approach; however the techniques I have described have worked and produced successful results for me in the typical working environment available to most amateur builders, so I include them in good faith. Before you start work on any of the projects described here please read the chapter on Health and Safety carefully so that you are familiar with the safe working practices. GRP materials, like many industrial chemicals, need careful use.

They can be messy and unpleasant, but when used correctly, glassfibre materials offer amateur users safe and simple methods of producing unique items ranging from a simple bonnet bulge to a complete car bodyshell. I hope you find this book interesting and informative to read but above all I hope it encourages you to try out some practical projects in GRP for yourself.

I replaced the steel monocoque chassis of my GTM Coupé with one made in glassfibre

01 GRP History
Where it all started

Glass Reinforced Plastic is a composite material utilising fine strands of glass, which are strong in tension, bound together in a solid plastic matrix which is strong in compression. The composite combines the best properties of both. The development of the composite obviously depended on the development of the two individual components which make it up. The ability to draw glass into fine fibres has been known since Roman times and cloth containing glass fibres as fine as silk was produced around the turn of the 19th century, but glassfibre as we know it was invented in 1938, originally as a material for use in heat insulation. Polyester resins, the most commonly used plastics, are petroleum based chemicals and the first patent, for a heat cured casting resin, appeared in 1933. Development of these materials was rapid and a suitable laminating resin quickly followed. The first practical use of GRP was to produce 'radomes' for wartime aircraft *(Pic 1)*.

A typical aircraft radome.

The aircraft radar aerials needed to be enclosed by a smooth fairing to protect and streamline them, but the material used had to allow the microwave radiation to pass through freely. Originally moulded plywood had been used, the plywood being formed in a concrete mould under pressure from inflatable air bags. This technique was obviously a forerunner of the vacuum bag system used in composite production today. Unfortunately the casein glues available at the time tended to absorb moisture and lose their strength. Mosquito aircraft, constructed in a similar way, suffered initially from the same problem until phenolic resin glues were used instead of caesin. GRP proved to be an ideal material for the radomes being light, strong and impervious to environmental conditions. In fact it is still used for this purpose today. The final step, from our point of view, came in 1946 when polyester resins containing styrene were produced. These could be cured at room temperature using an organic peroxide catalyst. This meant that specialist equipment was no longer needed and GRP fabrication was possible in a simple garage or workshop.

The first commercial application for the new material was in boatbuilding where its combination of strength, light weight, chemical stability and ease of use made it ideal for small and medium craft. These same properties also attracted the attention of the automotive enthusiasts. The first GRP bodied car, the Glasspar G2, was built (initially as a one off) in 1949 using a V8 engine and a Willys Jeep chassis *(Pic 2)*.

This ability to produce body panels without the need for heavy steel pressing equipment, tooling and jigs made it possible and practical for cars to be produced in small volumes or even as one-offs, and over the years hundreds of specialist car manufactures and individuals have used the technology. The advantages of GRP were not lost on the major manufacturers either, and as early as 1952 the huge Chevrolet Company used GRP to produce the body of the Corvette sports car (Pic 3). The choice of GRP was partly due to the difficulty of pressing sheet steel to the complex shapes required and partly due to the restrictive steel quotas still remaining after the war.

Ferrari produced its first GRP bodied production car, the 308 GTB, in 1975 but had been using the material in its racers well before this.

Some of the smaller specialist GRP car manufacturers eventually became well established companies too. TVR produced its first GRP bodied car, the Grantura (Pic 4), in 1958 and Ginetta made the G3 with a GRP body in 1959.

Lotus, always an innovator, took the use of GRP to a new level with the 1957 Elite by using the material to form a structural monocoque body with no separate chassis.

More recently companies such as Marcos, Midas and GTM (Pic 5) have followed this route and currently the kit car industry contains a mixture of those companies who use a structural GRP monocoque body/chassis unit and those who use an unstressed GRP bodyshell with a separate structural chassis. There are advantages and disadvantages to both methods of construction.

Technology never stands still and development of the products associated with GRP has continued over the years. There is now a wide choice of alternative fabrics such as Kevlar, Carbon Fibre, Twaron, Spectra polyethylene fibres and Astroquartz silica based fibres. Alternative resin systems now available include fire retardant polyesters, vinyl esters,

Where it all began. The Glasspar G2.

The Chevrolet Corvette was one of the first mass produced GRP bodies.

TVR always produced its cars in fibreglass, starting with the Grantura in 1958. This is a later TVR 3000M from the mid '70s.

epoxies and phenolics and they all offer increased performance or some specific advantage in properties. Some of these more exotic resins and fabrics need special techniques and conditions for successful use which are generally unavailable to the average amateur user. In this

This GTM Coupé uses a steel monocoque chassis with a fibreglass body lowered over the top and supplied in a pre-coloured gelcoat finish.

book I intend to concentrate on the materials which are easily available, relatively cheap, versatile, easy to use and give excellent result for the type of projects home users are likely to attempt. Generally these are the polyester resins and the glass based fabrics but, where appropriate, alternative materials will also be discussed. If they offer a mechanical or cosmetic advantage for the specific project you are planning then you need to be aware of them and of how they are used.

02 Materials And Tools

What's available

This chapter is intended simply as an introduction to some of the materials and tools you may come across in the production or repair of GRP mouldings and a brief description of how they are used. For more details of how to use them read through the chapters describing the various GRP projects. It is unlikely that you will ever need everything listed here. It really depends on how ambitious your projects are. Once you have tried a couple of simple jobs and have a better understanding of the products and their uses you will have a better idea of what will be required for a particular task.

Polyester lay-up resin

This is the resin most commonly used for laminating layers of glassfibre matting or cloth to produce the strong composite material suitable for boats, cars and all major GRP work. It is a sticky amber coloured liquid with the consistency of 10w-40 motor oil. It is slightly thickened so that even when working on

vertical surfaces sufficient resin will remain in the glassfibre to produce a strong structure. The resin will not set until a catalyst is added. The catalyst reacts with an accelerator already present in the resin, causing it to harden. Catalyst is normally added at the rate of about 2% (20ml in 1kg of resin). This gives the resin a pot life of around 20 minutes at 20°C. The resin can be coloured with pigments or metal powders if required.

Polyester gelcoat resin

This is a modified form of the resin. It is pale pink in colour and is much thicker (thixotropic). It barely pours and will not run, even on vertical surfaces. It uses the same catalyst in the same proportions as the lay-up resin. The catalyst is added and the gelcoat resin is brushed or sprayed into the mould to form a layer about 0.5mm thick and then allowed to harden. It is 'air inhibited' and stays sticky on the exposed surface so that the following layers will bond better. Glassfibre matting and lay-up

Polyester lay-up resin.

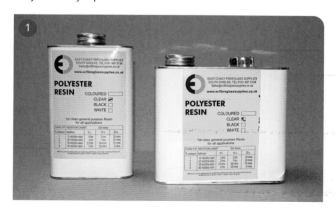

Polyester gelcoat resin.

resins are laminated onto the hardened gelcoat to form the load bearing structure. On the finished job the gelcoat forms the hard glossy outer surface. It needs to be water resistant and stable to UV light. As a guide to coverage 600g of gelcoat resin will cover an area of 1 m² to the correct depth *(Pic 2)*.

There is a further modified version of this resin designed specifically for gelcoat repairs. It is called gelcoat filler and is basically an extra thick gelcoat resin which can be tinted to match the original colour, then catalysed and used to fill cracks or scratches *(Pic 3)*.

Catalyst

The catalyst for polyester resins is Methyl Ethyl Ketone Peroxide (MEKP). All polyester resins must have catalyst added to start the hardening process. It is normally added at the rate of 2% by weight (20ml in 1Kg of resin). This can be reduced to a minimum of 1% if the resin is setting too quickly or increased to a maximum of 3% if the resin is setting too slowly at lower temperatures, but these limits must not be exceeded. The catalyst is corrosive and must be handled carefully *(Pic 4)*.

Vinylester resins

These resins offer better chemical resistance, better resistance to water ingress, better temperature stability and stronger bonding than polyester resins. This makes them ideal for the boatbuilding industry. In terms of cost they are around twice the price of polyesters and since, for our purposes, polyester resins are more than adequate, the extra cost of the vinylester resin is difficult to justify. If high performance resins are required for any reason, the modern epoxies are probably a better choice than vinylesters for automotive use.

Epoxy resins

These resins are much stronger than polyesters and offer far greater adhesion and chemical stability. Used with high performance fabrics such as Carbon Fibre and Kevlar they give excellent strength with low weight in structures used in aircraft, boats and cars. Originally epoxies needed high temperatures to cure them, making them unsuitable for amateur use, but recent developments have produced a hardener cured epoxy resin system which can be used in much the same way as polyester resin. The viscosity of the epoxy resin can be modified by adding filler powders and it can also be used as a strong gap-filling adhesive. Once again though, the extra cost of epoxy resins means that unless you really need their extra strength and durability they are an unnecessary luxury for most automotive use *(Pic 5)*.

Fillers

Various powders can be added to polyester resins to produce a thick paste suitable for use as filler *(Pic 6)*. Talc powder (right) is commonly used but alternatives include tiny glass

Gelcoat filler.

Epoxy resins.

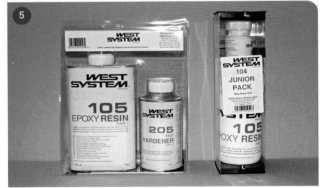

Catalyst.

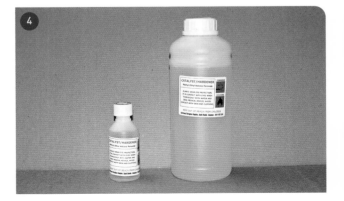

Fillers.

bubbles, for an ultra-lightweight filler, silica (centre), glassfibre strands (left) and carborundum grit, which produces a non-slip surface. The filler powder is mixed with the resin first to produce the paste then the hardener is stirred in just before use. Commercial body fillers use a different hardening system and the two are not interchangeable.

Chopped strand matt (CSM)

This is by far the most common reinforcing material used with polyester resin for hand lay-up *(Pic 7)*. It consists of 3–5cm long strands of glassfibre held together in a random arrangement by an emulsion or powder binder to form a mat. It is usually supplied on a roll 92cm wide and is sold by length, weight or area. The thickness of the matting is quoted as its weight per square metre and the commonly available thicknesses are 300g, 450g and 600g per m². Two layers of 300g matting would give a laminate the same thickness, strength and rigidity as one layer of 600g matting. In use, as the polyester resin is stippled into the matting, it dissolves the binder and the fibres become free to move and mould to the required shape. If epoxy resin is being used then powder-bound matting is essential. The binding emulsion normally used will not dissolve in epoxy resin so the matting does not wet out. Typically 1kg of CSM would need 2.5kg of lay-up resin to fully saturate it if a brush is used to apply the resin. If a paddle roller is used to consolidate the layers of matting,

slightly less resin is needed. 1kg of CSM would need about 2kg of resin when used with a roller.

Surface tissue

This is a fine glassfibre mat very similar to tissue paper *(Pic 8)*. It is supplied on a roll 1m wide and weighs only 25-30g per m². It adds no strength to the laminate but is used as a surfacing layer. During lamination it can be used to back-up the gelcoat to avoid air bubbles and voids or it can also be used to prevent the coarse pattern produced by CSM showing through the gelcoat. It can also be applied after the

Woven glassfibre fabric.

Chopped strand mat (CSM).

Fibreglass tape.

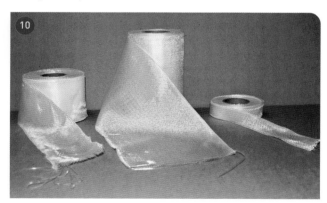

Surface tissue.

Fibreglass yarn.

final CSM layer to cover the rough glass strands and form a smooth surface. It needs 600g of resin to saturate 1m² of surface tissue.

Woven glassfibre fabric

As the name suggests these are cloth like materials made by weaving together long fine glassfibres (Pic 9). No binder is needed to hold the fibres in place. As with CSM they are supplied on rolls 1m wide and are available in various thicknesses from 300g - 1000g per m². They are also available in different weaves and fibre spacing. They drape better than CSM and add strength and stiffness to a moulding. The fibres do not consolidate together like those of CSM so adjacent layers of woven fabric do not bond together well. Glass fibre cloths are best used sandwiched between layers of CSM. 1kg of woven fabric will need about 1kg of resin to saturate it.

Fibreglass tape

This is simply woven fabric in tape form (Pic 10). The rolls can be obtained in various widths, thicknesses and weave patterns. Tape is convenient to use for small repairs or to reinforce stressed areas, such as mounting points, in a laminate.

There is also a fibreglass yarn made from very long fine glass fibres (Pic 11). It is used to reinforce internal corners where CSM or woven tape would lift away from the mould leaving a void or cavity.

Kevlar fabric

Kevlar was developed in 1965 by Du Pont. It was first used in the early 1970s to replace steel in racing tyres. It is a high performance polyaramid fabric which, weight for weight, is much stronger than glassfibre. Typically a Kevlar laminate can be almost half the weight of a GRP one for the same strength. Its drawbacks are the high cost of Kevlar and the difficulty of cutting the fabric. Only razor sharp blades or specialist shears work successfully. It is a bright yellow colour and available as a woven fabric (Pic 12) or as tape (Pic 13).

It works well with polyester resins but to make the best use

Carbon fibre fabric.

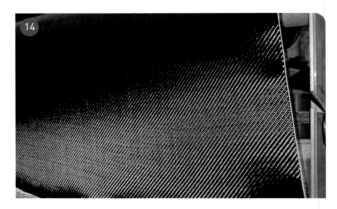

Carbon tape.

Carbon/kevlar weave.

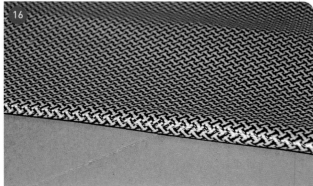

Kevlar fabric.

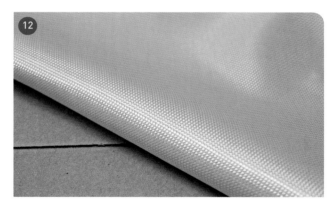

Kevlar tape.

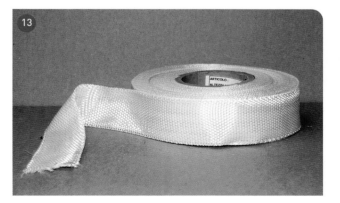

of its outstanding strength epoxy resins are ideal. Kevlar tape, trapped between layers of CSM, is very useful for reinforcing mounting points in a component.

Carbon fibre fabric

The first carbon fibre fabrics were woven in 1969 in the UK. Made from fibres containing microscopic graphite crystals, this black fabric offers twice the tensile strength of steel and equal stiffness but only quarter of the weight. Compared to fibreglass it has roughly the same tensile strength but is 10 times stiffer and about two-thirds of the weight. It is also an attractive fabric and, in spite of its high price, is being used to replace components purely for cosmetic reasons rather than for its mechanical properties. Commercially it is often supplied as 'Pre-preg', where the fabric is already saturated with heat curing epoxy resin for use in vacuum bag systems and pressurised autoclaves. Fortunately for us, it is also available as plain fabrics (Pic 14) and tapes (Pic 15) with different weights and weaves. As with Kevlar it will work well with polyester resins but for maximum strength it is best used with epoxy systems.

Combining the properties of both these materials there is a Carbon/Kevlar weave (Pic 16) . As with all the woven fabrics it is available in different weights and different weaves, some of which are cosmetically very striking. It offers a combination of the strength of Kevlar and the rigidity of Carbon Fibre.

Coremat

Coremat is a polyester sheet material that is used to add thickness, and therefore stiffness, to fibre reinforced laminates (Pic 17). It is available in a range of thicknesses from 1mm to 10mm. Coremat contains microspheres which prevent it absorbing large amounts of resin. Coremat which is 1mm thick will absorb only 600g of resin per m^2 compared to 1200g of resin for an equivalent thickness of CSM so there is a significant weight saving. Coremat has no inherent strength and must be sandwiched between two layers of CSM in a laminate.

Metal powders.

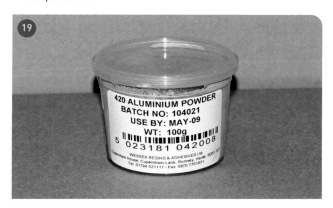

Coremat.

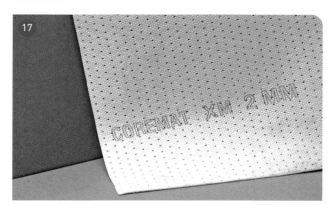

Rigid polyurethane foam sheet.

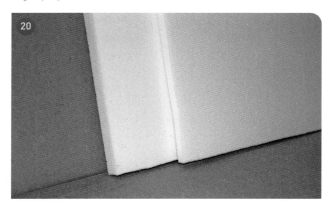

Pigment pastes, demonstrating how messy this process can be.

Two pack polyurethane foam mix.

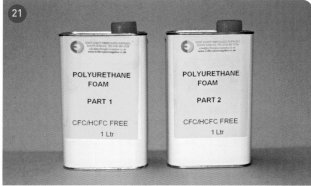

Pigment pastes

Pigments are available to colour the resins if required. They are incredibly dense colours and the tiniest amount can end up staining everything in sight, so handle them carefully. They tend to reduce the mechanical strength of the resin slightly, so no more pigment should be added than is necessary. For high load applications only the gelcoat should be tinted. They are used at the rate of 5% by weight for strong dark colours, up to a maximum of 10% for lighter colours. The pigment is added to the resin first and when fully mixed the catalyst is added and stirred in *(Pic 18)*.

Metal powders

A metallic finish can be produced by mixing metal powders with the resins. The process is called Cold Casting. The metal powder is added to the catalysed resin to produce a stiff paste. The paste is then brushed into the prepared mould replacing the normal gelcoat. When this has hardened, matting and resin are laminated onto it in the normal way and when the finished article is removed from the mould the outer surface can be polished to a soft lustre with fine wire wool and metal polish *(Pic 19)*.

Rigid polyurethane foam sheet

These sheets of rigid expanded closed cell foam are available in various thicknesses and can easily be cut and sanded to shape to make plugs, strengthening ribs or formers over which glassfibre can be laminated *(Pic 20)*. It is impervious to attack by polyester resins, unlike expanded polystyrene foam which dissolves instantly on contact. The foam is quite brittle and will break if bent beyond a gentle curve. There is a modified version called Scoreboard which has shallow slots cut into both sides of the sheet allowing it a greater degree of flexibility.

A two pack polyurethane foam mix is also available *(Pic 21)*. It is used to fill cavities and hollow sections. It gives strength and buoyancy. The two liquids are quickly stirred together and poured into the cavity. The foam expands to 20 times its original volume then slowly becomes rigid.

A flexible alternative to polyurethane foam is Ethafoam sheet. This is a flexible polyethylene foam sheet which is easy to cut and, unlike polyurethane sheet, can be bent into shape to produce ribs and formers. Ethafoam is also unaffected by polyester resins.

Polyvinyl alcohol (PVA)

This is the most common and straightforward release agent for amateur use *(Pic 22)*. It is a solution of PVA in alcohol and, as normally supplied, dries with a gloss finish. A less commonly used matt finish version is also available. It is normally tinted blue so that if you miss any areas they can be seen easily. The liquid can be brushed, sponged or sprayed onto the mould surface and then allowed to dry. It can be used over pre-waxed moulds providing the wax used is silicone free. Silicone waxes cause the PVA to 'bead' rather

Polyvinyl alcohol (PVA).

Polyester film.

Mould release wax.

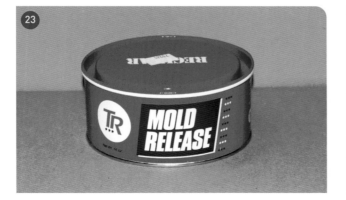

Brushes.

than to form an even film. It is also water soluble when wet or dry so water can be used to dissolve the film and aid difficult releases.

Mould release wax

Available as liquids or pastes these silicone free wax polishes are used to polish the mould surface to produce a high gloss finish and to provide an easier release *(Pic 23)*. 'Wax only' release systems, needing no PVA, are used by professionals but are really only effective after the mould has already been used with PVA several times. This limits their use for our purposes.

Aluminium fluted or paddle rollers.

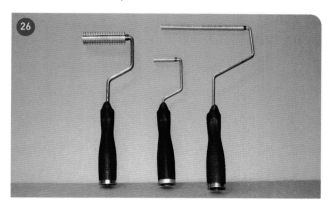

Narrow split type washer roller.

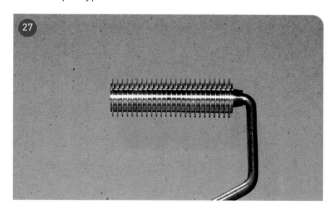

Containers.

Polyester film

This is a clear plastic film suitable for covering large flat surfaces. Resin will not stick to this material and, unlike polythene, it does not wrinkle on contact with resin. It can be taped on to a rigid backing material and used to make flat or single curvature GRP sheets. It can also be taped over gelcoat repairs to exclude air as they set and to form a smooth surface requiring less final finishing *(Pic 24)*.

Brushes

Expensive high quality brushes are not needed for GRP work.

Acetone.

Kleenall.

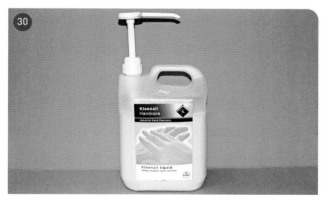

Rubber/polythene gloves.

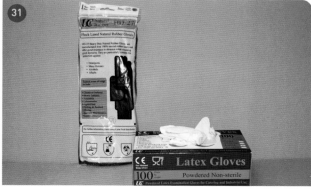

The main requirements are that the plastic handles do not dissolve in acetone or thinners and that they do not lose bristles in use. The odd bristle stuck in the main laminate will not be a problem but a loose bristle left in the gelcoat layer will be permanently visible in the outer surface and will be impossible to remove. The companies that supply the materials will also be able to supply suitable brushes. I tend to use ½", 1" and 2" brushes in most of my work *(Pic 25)*.

Rollers

For areas larger than about ¼m² you will get a better laminate and use less resin by using a roller to squeeze out any trapped air, force the resin into the matting and consolidate the layers of fibres. The cheapest and most commonly used rollers are the aluminium fluted or paddle type although others are available *(Pic 26/27)*. They can be bought in a variety of lengths and the very narrow single washer type is useful for forcing the matting into tight corners.

Containers

I have used a wide variety of containers, including aerosol can lids, take away food containers and Christmas pudding bowls, to mix up gelcoat and lay-up resins. Aluminium foil containers are fine as long as you don't puncture them with the mixing stick and, being disposable, don't need cleaning out when the job is finished. Plastic containers are also suitable providing the plastic doesn't react with the resin. Polythene and polypropylene are fine but polystyrene turns to a sticky mess very quickly on contact with polyester resins. Test the container first before you pour in a large quantity of resin. Not surprisingly, you can buy suitable containers, with tight fitting lids, from the same companies that sell you the resins and matting *(Pic 28)*.

Acetone/thinners

I threw away a lot of brushes and containers until I found out that uncured resin can be cleaned out by dissolving it in acetone or cellulose thinners. Acetone is more effective but cellulose thinners is generally easier to obtain locally. Neither of these should be used for cleaning resin from hands as they remove natural oils from the skin and can cause dermatitis. They should also be kept in covered containers as they evaporate quickly and they are both highly flammable *(Pic 29)*.

Kleenall

This is a water washable hand cleaner which can remove even set resin from skin. It is available as a paste or a liquid. It will also remove oil, grease, adhesives and oil based or cellulose paint *(Pic 30)*.

Rubber/polythene gloves

The best way to protect your hands is not to get resin on them in the first place. Boxes of disposable rubber or polythene gloves are readily available and I use them every time I work with GRP. Latex rubber gloves are easier to work in but they dissolve very quickly in acetone or thinners. Polythene gloves last a little longer in cleaning solvents but tend to be more awkward in use. Marigold type rubber gloves tend to be tougher and resist solvents better but are more expensive initially. If you can find them, PVC gloves are better still as they are unaffected by solvents *(Pic 31)*.

If you have a look at the product catalogue of a typical GRP supplier you will see that the list above is by no means extensive. What I have tried to do is to include those materials which you are likely to come across and possibly use in typical home fabrication or repair applications. I have also tried to give you enough information to enable you to decide whether a particular material is necessary or even suitable for the use you have in mind. If you find this list daunting or confusing have a look at a couple of the projects in the following chapters. They will give you a good idea of the materials and tools which could be considered to be essential and those which may initially be thought of as luxuries.

03 Workshop

Sorting the workplace

In an ideal world we would all have immaculate, clinically clean, air conditioned workshops like those used by the modern F1 teams. In reality all my work is done in a single car garage attached to a standard semi-detached house. I have no space for a permanent workbench and only limited storage space for materials. In spite of this I have built major body panels and even a complete GRP car chassis in this working area *(Pic 1)*.

Apart from adequate working space, the most important factors for successful GRP work are temperature and humidity. The resins used in glassfibre work are designed to cure at around 18–20°C. It is possible to adjust the amount of hardener used slightly to compensate for small temperature variations but this is not ideal. Too much moisture in the atmosphere can also cause curing problems or wrinkling of the gelcoat. If you are in no rush and are prepared to wait for the one warm dry day we get here in the UK every Summer then you can work with the garage doors open and no additional heat required, but don't work in direct sunlight. The UV light causes the resin to set much quicker than normal. For the rest of the year you will have to find some other way of producing a warm dry atmosphere. If you have mains power in your working area, then a free standing oil-filled radiator, convector heater or fan heater is ideal *(Pic 2)*.

The heater should be used to pre-heat the working area and then to maintain the temperature until the laminating process is complete and the resin is cured. Many of these heaters have built in thermostats which keep the temperature constant and save energy. If you do not have mains power in your workshop then your options are more limited. A gas powered space heater or a paraffin heater can be used but since they both use naked flames they must be turned off whilst the actual laminating process is taking place as the resin is highly flammable. They can be turned on

My working area.

This is the fan heater I use in my garage.

again once the laminating is complete and all flammable resins and solvents have been safely stored away. You must also ensure that your workspace is well ventilated if you use either of these options as they use up the available oxygen in the air to burn their fuel and, as a by-product of combustion, generate a large amount of water vapour too. Space heaters and fan heaters will also blow dust into the air which may settle on your laminate, so either switch them on well in advance to ensure that no free dust remains or switch them off whilst the actual laminating is taking place. This is particularly important for the gelcoat layer.

Nothing special is needed in terms of lighting. Two or three fluorescent tubes should be fine in a normal sized garage. All you need to be able to do is inspect surface finishes for imperfections and to spot air bubbles or dry patches in laminations. If your current lighting set up is bright enough to allow you to do this then it should be OK. I have a 500w floodlight which I sometimes use but this is more as a source of additional heat rather than light.

It is possible to work on the garage floor but I have found that as I get older this option becomes less practical. I spend more time getting up and down that I do actually working with the glassfibre. It is also possible to laminate with the resin brush in one hand and the workpiece in the other but this too is far from ideal. A simple flat working area is perfect for measuring and mixing resins, cutting out matting and supporting work whilst laminating. My temporary bench is based on an old and well used Black & Decker Workmate *(Pic 3)* .

I also have a piece of MDF about 1200mmx600mmx19mm with a baton screwed down the centre *(Pic 4)*.

I clamp the baton in the workbench to give a large secure working area. GRP work is messy, so I cover the MDF with a disposable surface. You can use lining wallpaper, polythene sheet from garden centres or even wheelie bin liners taped into place *(Pic 5)*.

Once the covers become too messy they can be discarded and replaced. The bench itself can be protected in the same way, as can the floor area around your working space. If you are a really messy worker you could also protect the walls in a similar way.

For waste disposal I have a black bin liner taped to the wall. Once it fills up I remove it, seal it and dispose of the whole thing without needing to open it *(Pic 6)*.

Materials storage is basically common sense. The liquid materials need to be stored at room temperature or slightly below. The resins do gradually deteriorate with age. The curing times become shorter and eventually the whole lot will set solid in the container, so try not to buy any more resin than you will use to complete the current project. They are flammable, so keep them away from ignition sources

My long suffering Black & Decker Workmate bench.

The bench ready for use with its disposable covering.

This MDF sheet is clamped in the bench to form the working surface.

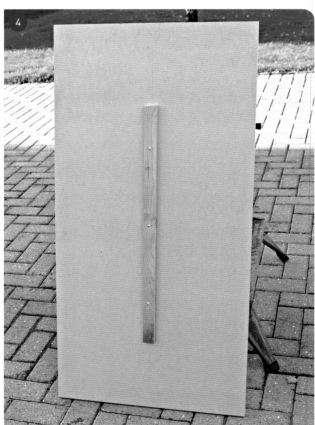

and direct heat. They are also poisonous so they must be out of reach of children and pets. Catalyst should not be stored with the resin or any other flammable materials and if you also have a stock of accelerator, this should not be stored with the catalyst. Glassfibre sheet, tape and fabric can be stored flat or on a roll but must be covered with a polythene or similar sheet to prevent dust contamination. Dusty matting can be difficult to wet out and can contaminate the laminate later on.

As you can see, very little specialist equipment is needed to work with GRP and this is one of its major advantages over other materials for amateur builders and fabricators. High quality components can be produced in domestic garages or workshops without a large financial outlay.

The plastic liner which I use as a disposable waste bin.

Hints & tips

• Have the right safety equipment to hand and plan ahead

Please read this chapter carefully before you begin any sort of practical GRP work. I have no wish to frighten anyone away from working with glassfibre products and, if you are aware of potential hazards and take sensible precautions, these materials are perfectly safe to use. If you fully understand the materials you are working with you are far less likely to have an accident in the first place. Should the worst happen, however, then you need to be fully aware of the correct action to take before, rather than after, it happens. There is rarely time to consult the safety sheets once the accident is actually taking place.

Most of the liquids used in GRP work are produced from petroleum extracts and are therefore generally flammable, poisonous and harmful to eyes and skin. There are some simple rules for the safe use of polyester resins and their associated products.

• **Do not smoke or use naked flames in the working area**
• **Do not let any materials contact the skin, eyes or mouth**
• **Wear gloves or barrier cream and use eye protection**
• **Do not inhale any vapours**
• **Work in a well ventilated area**

It is not a good idea to have any food or drink in the working area. Sooner or later you will end up contaminating either the workpiece or your mug of tea and neither option is to be recommended. The following paragraphs outline the specific hazards and treatments associated with the main chemicals used in GRP work.

Polyester resins

These are flammable liquids and can actually ignite spontaneously through heat build up if a large quantity is allowed to set in a container. Spread unused catalysed resin over a large area to prevent heat build up. Should resin catch fire do not use water. Use a Halon, Foam, CO_2 or Dry Powder extinguisher *(Pic 1)*.

A fire extinguisher is cheap to buy.

The resin also gives off harmful fumes as it sets. There should be no problem if adequate ventilation is provided but if drowsiness is experienced move the affected person from the exposure area into the fresh air until it clears.

Resin in the eye must be washed out thoroughly with an eye bath *(Pic 2)* or running water for at least 15 minutes and medical advice should be sought.

If resin is swallowed rinse out the mouth and drink plenty of water or milk. Keep the person under observation. Do not induce vomiting. Seek medical advice.

Resin on the skin can be removed using Kleenall cream or liquid. If these are not available flush the area well with soap and water. Spillages can be absorbed using sand, earth or soak granules.

MEKP hardener

This is perhaps the nastiest of the chemicals associated with GRP work. It is highly corrosive and therefore must not be allowed to contact the skin, eyes or mouth. It is also flammable and, in addition, as it burns it releases oxygen causing the fire to burn more fiercely. It should not be stored with resins or other flammable materials. In case of fire the best material to use is water. Other extinguishers are less effective due to the oxygen being produced by the hardener itself.

If the fumes are inhaled remove the victim from the

Resin in the eye must be washed out thoroughly.

exposure area, to an open area with fresh air. Seek medical help immediately.

Hardener in the eye must be washed out thoroughly with an eye bath or running water for at least 15 minutes and medical advice should be sought.

If hardener is swallowed rinse out the mouth and drink plenty of water or milk. Keep the person under observation. Do not induce vomiting as this may be a breathing hazard. Seek medical advice.

For skin contact remove any contaminated clothing and rinse the skin with running water for 15 minutes. Seek medical help. Spillages can be washed away with water.

Accelerator

Most resins come with the accelerator already added so there is no reason why you should ever need to use the undiluted product however, if you do, the most important rule by far is never mix undiluted accelerator and MEKP hardener together. An explosion can occur. Accelerator and hardener should never even be stored together. The hazards associated with the accelerator are very similar to those of the hardener. It is in a flammable solvent and can also cause chemical skin burns. Should the accelerator catch fire you can use water, Halon, Foam, CO_2 or Dry Powder extinguishers.

If the fumes are inhaled remove the victim from the exposure area, to an open area with fresh air. Seek medical help immediately.

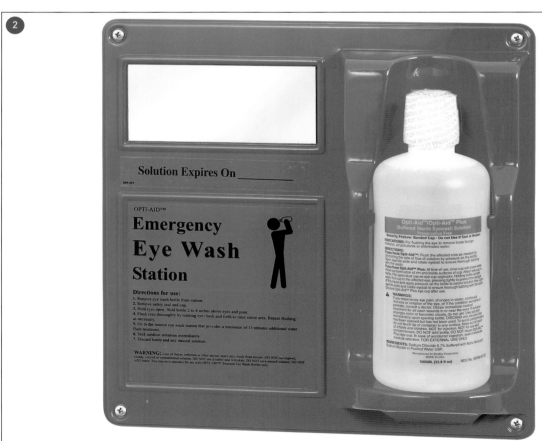

Accelerator in the eye must be washed out thoroughly with an eye bath or running water for at least 15 minutes and medical advice should be sought.

If accelerator is swallowed rinse out the mouth and drink plenty of water or milk. Keep the person under observation. Do not induce vomiting as this may be a breathing hazard. Seek medical advice.

For skin contact remove any contaminated clothing and rinse the skin with running water for 15 minutes. Seek medical help. Spillages can be absorbed using sand, earth or soak granules.

PVA release agent

The hazards associated with this material come mainly from the solvent, which is an alcohol and is therefore flammable. It is less harmful than some of the previous chemicals, being an irritant rather than corrosive, but some precautions are still required. In case of fire Halon, Foam, CO_2 or Dry Powder extinguishers are suitable.

Inhaling the fumes may irritate the respiratory tract but drowsiness is unlikely unless the concentration is very high. If it does occur move the victim to an open area with fresh air.

Swallowing the liquid may cause vomiting or diarrhoea. Drink plenty of water or milk. Seek medical advice.

Any PVA spilled on the skin can be washed off safely with soapy water.

Spillages can be rinsed away with water or absorbed using sand, earth or soak granules.

Glassfibre matting

Glass fibres are actually used to produce fireproof fabrics so there is no fire hazard associated with CSM.

There is no danger from inhalation or swallowing either unless you manage to swallow enough to actually block up your digestive system.

In case of eye contact do not rub the eyes. Rinse thoroughly with cold water for at least 15 minutes.

In use, some skin irritation may occur as the tiny glass fibres stick into the skin. Do not rub or scratch these areas. Wash them thoroughly with cold soapy water and a cloth to remove the fibres. Do not use warm water. It will open the pores of the skin causing the fibres to penetrate deeper.

When cutting, grinding or sanding the finished GRP product there is the usual dust hazard but this dust is particularly nasty as it will contain fine glass particles. A facemask and eye protection (Pic 3) should always be worn under these circumstances.

Acetone/cellulose thinners

These are extremely flammable liquids with very low flash points so they ignite easily even at room temperature. They are also powerful grease solvents and will remove the natural grease from skin very quickly causing dermatitis or cracking of the skin. Use PVC gloves rather than latex if you can find them. They will dissolve many plastics so store them

only in the containers in which they were supplied to you. They will irritate the eyes, throat, lungs and digestive tract so be very careful when handling these liquids.

Acetone fires can be extinguished using water, Halon, Foam, CO_2 or Dry Powder.

Water must not be used on fires involving thinners but Halon, Foam, CO_2 or Dry Powder extinguishers can be used.

If the fumes from either product are inhaled remove the victim from the exposure area, to an open area with fresh air. Seek medical help immediately.

Either liquid in the eye must be washed out thoroughly with an eye bath or running water for at least 15 minutes and medical advice should be sought.

If Acetone or thinners are swallowed rinse out the mouth and throat thoroughly. Seek medical advice.

In case of skin contact remove all contaminated clothes immediately unless stuck to the skin. Wash immediately with plenty of soap and water. Spillages can be absorbed using sand, earth or soak granules.

2-pack polyurethane foam

The two liquids used are flammable and give off harmful vapours. One of the components is an isocyanate and great care must be taken to avoid breathing this vapour. The first symptom of exposure is irritation of the respiratory tract but drowsiness and even unconsciousness can result from excessive exposure. Always work in a well ventilated room or in the open air.

In case of fire use a Halon, CO_2 or Dry Powder extinguisher.

Medical aid should also be obtained if excessive inhalation occurs or if any material is swallowed.

If the foam mix is in contact with the skin or eyes, flush immediately, with copious amount of water. Spillages can be absorbed using sand, earth or soak granules.

Once the two components are mixed and poured a chemical reaction causes them to foam. Heat is generated and more harmful vapours are produced. Once again work in a well ventilated area. Do not let any of the mixture touch your skin. It may be hot enough to burn you and it will stick tenaciously. Try to wash it off before it sets or it will be very difficult to remove from the skin.

Use a facemask and eye protection when cutting fibreglass.

Planning

As you read through the hazards and treatments detailed above you will notice that many of the recommendations are common to a number of materials so it is well worth dealing with them at the workshop planning stage. In particular ventilation of the working area is essential since most materials give off harmful vapours. Fire extinguishers are not expensive and one of the recommended types should also be in easy reach when you are working. An eye wash kit would be a good idea too although current thinking is that unless the water in the kit is changed frequently to avoid infection you are probably better off with a simple flexible tube attached to a slow-running cold water tap. A bucket full of sand or some soak granules will deal with most spills and a black bin liner taped to the wall makes an ideal disposable waste container.

Hopefully, once you understand the hazards associated with these materials you will handle and use them safely and you will never need to use most of the information in this chapter but please make sure you have read and understood it all before you move on.

Have a first aid kit in the workplace at all times.

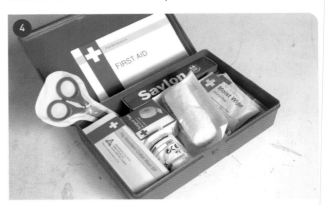

05 Producing GRP Sheet

A simple project to start

The easiest way to learn how to fabricate in GRP is to use it to actually make something useful. Flat sheets of GRP can be very useful in automotive work. They can be used for brackets, shields, inner wings and interior trim panels. They are strong, light, and flexible. They can be self coloured, will not corrode and are impervious to water. As an illustration of what can be achieved I built a complete replacement chassis/tub for my GTM Coupe kit car using large flat GRP panels bonded and laminated together *(Pic 1)*.

The commonly available Contiplas type white melamine laminated chipboard makes an excellent former for flat sheets of GRP. If treated properly it can be re-used many times *(Pic 2)*.

The surface needs to be grease free and dry or the PVA release agent will not spread evenly. Clean the surface with detergent and water and dry it thoroughly *(Pic 3)*.

You can use release wax if you wish but I have not found it necessary with this material. The PVA can be sprayed, brushed or applied with a sponge. A thin even coating is

A sheet of melamine faced board ready for use.

The bulkhead and footwell area of my GTM chassis.

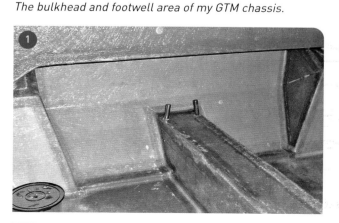

Wiping the sheet with water and detergent to remove grease.

required and personally I find this easiest to achieve with a sponge. Pour some of the PVA liquid into a saucer or shallow dish and dip in the sponge (Pic 4)

Remove the excess liquid and spread the PVA in long straight lines over the surface (Pic 5).

Don't allow the liquid to build up in ridges. They will show up in the GRP surface, as will any other surface imperfection no matter how small. Make sure the whole surface is fully covered. If you miss even the smallest spot the GRP will stick to the laminate and both surfaces will be ruined. When the whole area is covered with a thin even layer allow it to dry thoroughly (Pic 6). Pour any excess PVA back into the container and wash the sponge and dish with warm soapy water.

Make sure the conditions in your working area, especially the temperature, are suitable before you go any further.

Next you need to work out how much gelcoat resin you will need. Roughly work out the area you intend to cover. This sheet is 600mm x 450mm which works out at 0.27m². 600g of gelcoat resin will cover an area of one square metre to the correct thickness, so this sheet will need 600 x 0.27 which is 162g of gelcoat resin. Weigh out the correct amount of resin into a polythene or metal container. Don't mix up too much – it will simply be wasted and you will have more cleaning up to do. In this case 180g will give a small margin for error without producing much waste. I have an old set of kitchen scales which I use exclusively for GRP work. Don't borrow the good ones – they will be wrecked within minutes no matter how careful you try to be (Pic 7).

The gelcoat does not have to be coloured but it makes it much easier to see how even the coating is when you are applying it. Dark colours are used at the rate of 5%, which is 5g in 100g of resin. Lighter colours need more than this but don't exceed 10% whatever you do as the resin properties deteriorate beyond this point. The 180g of resin being used here will need 9g of pigment for a 5% mix. For convenience this is roughly two teaspoons (Pic 8).

The board coated with release agent ready for use.

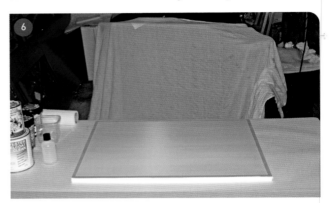

Pouring the PVA into a suitable container.

Weighing out the gelcoat resin.

Using a sponge to spread the PVA onto the surface.

Measuring out the pigment using a teaspoon.

Stir the pigment into the resin slowly but thoroughly (Pic 9). Don't mix in any air bubbles. They may show up as pinholes in the final surface.

If you are making a number of panels and you want the colour to be consistent for each one then you should mix up all the gelcoat resin for the whole batch in one go. Add catalyst only to the amount you are using immediately and store the rest in a sealed container.

Carefully measure out the catalyst. Don't be tempted to add extra catalyst – it can affect the properties of the resin and cause dangerous heat build up. It can also cause the gelcoat to separate from the mould prematurely. The correct rate is 2% by weight. Small weights don't show up too well on kitchen scales, so it's easier to measure the catalyst by volume. Fortunately 1ml of catalyst weighs about 1g so the conversion is easy. In practical terms then, you need to add 2ml of catalyst for every 100g of resin. If you can get hold of a small measuring cylinder, that would be perfect but the small polythene measuring cups provided with some medicines and plant insecticides will also work well. They are available new from pharmacists too. A set of kitchen measuring spoons marked in ml can also be used although metal ones will last longer than plastic with the harsh cleaning solvents used (Pic 10).

A teaspoon holds about 5ml so if all else fails you could simply use one of those.

If you need to adjust the setting speed of the resin you can reduce the amount of catalyst to a minimum of 1% or increase it to a maximum of 3% but don't go outside these limits. The 180g of resin being used here will need 3.6g of catalyst or just less than one teaspoon (Pic 11).

Pour the catalyst into the resin and mix it in slowly but thoroughly. If the catalyst is not fully mixed the resin may set unevenly. It may harden too quickly in some areas and not at

Measuring out the hardener using a teaspoon.

Stirring the pigment slowly into the resin.

Stirring the hardener slowly into the resin.

Alternative measuring devices for the MEKP hardener.

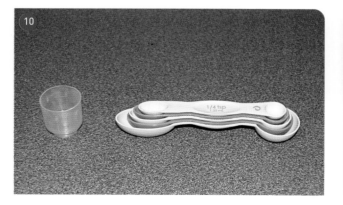

Painting the tinted and catalysed gelcoat onto the prepared surface.

all in others. Stir the catalyst in slowly so that you do not form air bubbles in the gelcoat resin (Pic 12). They can form pinholes in the surface of the final laminate.

Using a suitably sized paintbrush, paint the resin onto the PVA surface. Don't try to 'stretch' the resin as you would with paint. Fully load the brush and spread the resin out to form an even coating about 0.5mm thick (Pic 13).

If you have coloured the resin you will be able to see how consistent the thickness is. You should have 15 – 20 minutes working time if the temperature is correct (Pic 14).

If the resin starts to set as you are painting it on stop at once! The resin will always set faster in the container than it does on the work piece due to heat build up, so quickly finish working with the resin already on the surface then clean out the tools and container.

Wipe out any excess resin from the container and brush with old newspaper and clean them with acetone or thinners. The most effective cleaning system uses two pots of solvent (Pic 15). Pot one is used first and removes the bulk of the resin from the brush and container. Agitate the brush in the solvent then squeeze out as much liquid as possible with paper towel. Move on to pot two. The solvent in pot two removes the small amount of resin left behind from pot one. Once again agitate the brush in the solvent and squeeze out as much liquid as possible then leave the tools to dry thoroughly.

Eventually the liquid in pot one becomes saturated with resin and needs replacing. Dispose of this liquid responsibly. At this point pot two becomes pot one and what used to be pot one is now filled with clean solvent and becomes pot two. Easy isn't it? The two containers need to have tight fitting lids or the liquids will quickly evaporate away. After cleaning the tools all traces of acetone or thinners have to dry out fully or the cleaning solvents will contaminate the resin the next time they are used.

At 20°C the gelcoat resin on the work piece should start to set after about 30 minutes but it must be fully set before we can laminate onto it. The resin is 'air inhibited' and will stay sticky on the exposed surface even when fully set. This helps the subsequent layers to stick to it. If we laminate onto the gelcoat before it is sufficiently set the new resin can attack it and cause it to wrinkle. Touch the resin gently with your finger. It should feel sticky to the touch but no resin should come off onto your finger. Once again this will be easier to see if you have coloured the resin.

This next step is optional but I always include it and I would advise you to do so too until you become more experienced at laminating. The gelcoat is covered with a layer of surface tissue and lay-up resin. This avoids unsupported gelcoat caused by voids or air bubbles in the CSM layers. These voids show up on the outer surface as slightly raised blisters which

The finished gelcoat surface.

Weighing out the lay-up resin for the surface tissue layer.

The two pot cleaning system using polythene ice cream containers.

Stirring the pigment into the lay-up resin.

can be pushed in but spring back again. If you break this gelcoat bubble the void beneath can be clearly seen. By laminating a layer of surface tissue onto the gelcoat it will be supported and will not lift even if small air bubbles remain under the CSM layers. Cut a piece of surface tissue large enough to cover the area of the gelcoat resin. Weigh out sufficient lay-up resin to saturate the tissue. It needs 600g of resin for 1m² of tissue. This is the same rate of coverage as the gelcoat resin so the same amount is needed, in this case 180g *(Pic 16)*.

You can tint this layer of resin too if you want the final surface colour to be more consistent or denser. The pigment is added in the same proportions as for the gelcoat resin and stirred in thoroughly. The stirring can be more vigorous here as the presence of tiny air bubbles makes no difference *(Pic 17)*.

The catalyst (3.6ml again) can then be added as before and stirred in thoroughly *(Pic 18)*.

Paint a thin coat of resin onto the gelcoat *(Pic 19)*. Lay the tissue carefully in place *(Pic 20)*. The rest of the resin is now stippled into the tissue until it is fully saturated and there are no air bubbles trapped between the tissue and the gel. Don't try to brush the resin on with a sideways motion or you will tear the tissue *(Pic 21)*.

When you've finished, wipe away any excess resin and clean the container and brush as described earlier *(Pic 22)*.

When this layer has set we can finally laminate on the layers of CSM which give the panel its structure and strength. The grade of matting used is entirely up to you. It may seem that the thinner matting is more flexible and will form round curves easier but in fact, once the resin has dissolved the binder and the fibres are free to move, there is no difference at all. I tend to use the thickest 600g matting simply because I am used to working with it and I can control the final thickness of the panel better. As a rough guide, the gelcoat and tissue layer will be about 1mm thick and each additional layer of laminated 600g matting will add

Carefully laying the surface tissue onto the wet resin.

Adding the catalyst for the lay-up resin.

Wetting out the surface tissue. Don't tear it.

Painting a thin coat of lay-up resin onto the hardened gelcoat.

Check for any air bubbles or dry patches before the resin sets.

a further 1mm to the overall thickness. This sample sheet will be made up of gelcoat, tissue and two layers of laminated 600g matting and will end up about 3mm thick.

The CSM needs to be big enough to overlap the panel by about 2cm on each edge. On this small panel each layer can be made from one piece of matting. You can join smaller pieces together if you do not have whole pieces large enough to cover the area, but the thickness of the final panel is more difficult to control this way. When you join pieces of matting try to overlap torn edges of matting rather than cut edges. They will merge without a step or ledge. Pieces should overlap each other by about 5cm. To work out how much resin to mix up you need to know the total weight of the matting you will be using. You can work it out from the area and the grade of matting used or, like me, you can weight it on your newly stolen scales. In this case the two pieces of CSM weigh about 400g. If we are not using a roller to apply the resin, the weight needed is 2.5 times the weight of the matting. This gives us a weight of 1000g of lay-up resin needed. I will be using a roller to laminate the panel, so less resin is used. Typically the weight of resin required when a roller is used is roughly twice the weight of the CSM so only 800g of resin is needed.

It is very tempting to simply weigh the total amount of resin required into your container, add the catalyst and start laminating but...

Weighing out a larger amount of resin to laminate the CSM.

Measuring out the catalyst using a medicine cup.

1. Remember that the resin will set much quicker in the larger quantities in the container. Until you have some experience of the setting times and can work fairly quickly, I suggest that you only mix up a maximum of 500g at a time or you may end up with a pot of solid overheated resin giving off acrid choking smoke. I know this from experience.

2. To avoid excess heat build up, which may distort the panel; it is not advisable to laminate more than two layers at a time. Allow for this when you mix up the resin. If you want a thicker laminate, more layers can be added once the first ones are set.

Painting a thin coat of resin onto the surface.

Positioning the CSM matting carefully to overlap the edges.

Quickly stippling the resin into the matting.

You can actually use pigment in the resin used at this stage too, so that the whole panel will be completely self coloured. I would advise against this though, until you have more experience of laminating, as colouring the resin makes it more difficult to see whether the CSM matting has been completely saturated (wetted out). Air bubbles are not easy to see if the resin is coloured.

The actual laminating process is fairly straightforward. Weigh out your resin and add the catalyst at the rate of 2% (Pic 23).

A batch of 500g of resin will need 10ml of catalyst. This time I am using a medicine cup to measure the catalyst (Pic 24). Stir it in well, then paint a thin coat of resin onto the work (Pic 25). Carefully place the layer of matting onto the job (Pic 26).

Transfer the resin onto the matting quickly to avoid it setting in the pot then, using a stippling action with the brush, saturate the whole piece of matting with resin (Pic 27).

Use a vertical action to avoid pulling the glass fibres

The matting turns translucent when it is wetted out completely.

Rolling the whole area to squeeze the resin through the matting.

Laying the second layer of CSM over the first.

Rolling the surface again at 90° to the original direction.

Stippling the resin into the second layer.

When you finish laminating check the whole area for bubbles or dry spots.

sideways and creating thinner areas. The white matting will turn translucent as it is soaked in resin and any dry patches or air bubbles can be seen easily. Make sure the matting is fully saturated right to the edges of the panel (Pic 28).

When you are sure the first layer of matting is completely wetted out you can lay on the second layer and simply repeat the process (Pic 29).

If you run out of resin, just mix up some more and continue

working. You do not need to clean the brush or container until you are finished laminating (Pic 30).

Once all the resin has been added it is time to use the roller to force the resin into the matting and to consolidate the layers and any overlaps. Until you actually use a roller it is difficult to believe how quick and effective they are. Make sure the roller spins feely or it will drag the matting. Use very gentle pressure at first and roll back and forth along the

Sanding the laminate with 80 grit abrasive to remove sharp stray fibres.

Most of the PVA has stuck to the GRP but it peels or washes off easily.

Lifting the laminate at one corner to start the separation.

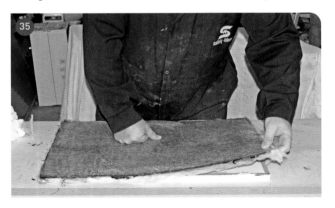

Use a fine tooth blade suitable for cutting steel. GRP will quickly blunt wood tools.

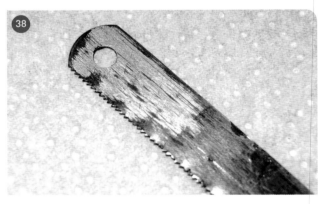

The sheet should peel away from the board easily.

These are Tungsten Carbide grit coated blades. They work well with GRP.

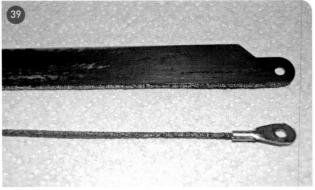

whole length of the panel increasing the pressure as the resin penetrates the matting (Pic 31).

Dry areas will quickly disappear and the resin will squeeze through the whole thickness of the laminate. Roll the whole panel again at 90° to the original direction (Pic 32).

By now the panel should be fully wetted out, but if there are any areas which need more work the roller will quickly sort them out. Once you are happy that the whole panel is fully saturated, dispose of any unused resin and clean out the tools and container (Pic 33).

You can add more layers once these have set if required, but to avoid heat build up limit yourself to two layers at a time. Although the catalysed resin sets fairly quickly it continues to cure for quite some time afterwards. The curing can take 24 hours at 20°C or a few days if the temperature is low. Until the resin is fully cured, the moulding is referred to as 'green' and must not be removed from the mould or former as it can distort.

When our flat sheet of GRP has fully cured it can be peeled from the Contiboard. Before you attempt to handle the newly moulded GRP, take some 80 grit production paper and rub over the whole surface (Pic 34) to remove any stray glass fibres which, now they are coated in resin, are incredibly sharp and will easily penetrate skin.

To release the sheet from the panel, start at one corner and carefully lift the GRP (Pic 35).

If you did a good job with the PVA, the sheet should simply peel away (Pic 36).

If you need to use some leverage try using a piece of plastic such as the spreader supplied with body filler or a plastic ruler. Metal will scratch both surfaces very easily. Pieces of hardboard can be used as wedges too. If all else fails lift one corner and carefully pour water between the two surfaces. It will gradually dissolve the PVA film. You can see that in this case the PVA has remained on the GRP. It is a thin but tough film (Pic 37).

The sheet can be trimmed at the edges to remove the rough matting. A simple hacksaw or pad saw with a hacksaw blade can be used to cut the GRP but use a fine toothed blade to avoid splintering (Pic 38).

I have also had good results using the tungsten carbide grit coated cutting tools (Pic 39).

Be sure to cut downwards through the gelcoat to avoid it splintering away from the matting. The cut on the left (Pic 40) was made this way but the cut on the right was made from the CSM side of the laminate and the gelcoat has splintered badly.

An electric jig saw can be used but since they cut on the up stroke of the blade they must be used from the rear of the sheet to correctly cut through the gelcoat and avoid splintering.

The gel coat has splintered badly on the cut made from the CSM side of the sheet.

Removing the sharp edges and fibres with 80 grit abrasive paper.

Sawing down through the gelcoat to avoid splintering.

The finished panel with the same surface finish as the original melamine board.

My favourite cutting tool for GRP is an angle grinder with a thin cutting disc fitted. This cuts quickly through the material and does the least damage to the laminate as it cuts. It is also really the only way to cut through Kevlar laminates without causing the fabric to fray. Unfortunately it also produces large amounts of dust. Since I am working inside on this example, I am using a grit blade in a sheet hacksaw to trim the edges *(Pic 41)*.

Whatever cutting tool you use you must avoid breathing the dust or getting it in your eyes. It is basically powder glass mixed with polyester resin dust. Neither of these is to be recommended in eyes or lungs.

The cut edges can still be sharp, so a final rub down with coarse abrasive paper on a sanding block will remove any remaining rough edges *(Pic 42)*.

After trimming the GRP sheet, both surfaces can be cleaned with warm soapy water to remove any remaining PVA release agent. The final surface finish is a soft sheen which is identical to the finish on the laminate board used as the former *(Pic 43)*.

The flat sheet you have produced can be cut to shape, joined and bonded with GRP strips to produce battery boxes, panels and so on.

The aim of this simple project has been to demonstrate the basic materials and techniques used in GRP lamination. The other projects in the book build on and extend these techniques and use them to copy, fabricate or repair a variety of automotive components. I am sure you will find something in there which fires your imagination or encourages you to try your hand at component fabrication.

06 Replica Panels & Mould Making

Creating an accurate copy

One of the most useful aspects of GRP is its ability to make detailed, accurate moulds and to be able to produce exact

The repaired and re-shaped hugger being used as the plug.

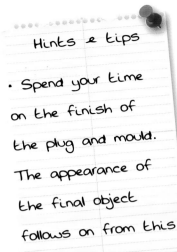

Primer and spray putty are used to fill fine marks and scratches.

copies of objects or panels from these moulds. GRP can no longer be used to replace structural panels in road going vehicles but boot lids, bonnets, scoops and bulges can all be made in lightweight corrosion free glassfibre. It is important to realise at the outset that the surface finish on your replica panel can never be any better than that of the original object, known as the plug, and any surface imperfections will also be faithfully reproduced on your replica. The more time you spend getting a good finish on the plug the less time you will have to spend on the mould and the finished replica. The materials used are not important. Only the shape and surface finish matter when making the mould.

To illustrate this project I am producing a replica of a GRP rear hugger for my BMW motorcycle. The original did not fit particularly well and was damaged when it made contact with the rear wheel. To avoid this problem in the future I intend to modify the shape slightly and to add reinforcement to the replica as needed. Using commercial body filler and hardboard the damage is repaired, the shape is modified slightly and large surface imperfections are filled *(Pic 1)*.

Spray putty and filler primer are used to fill fine marks and scratches *(Pic 2)*. To make the plug easy to hold, a piece of wood is temporarily glued to the inside using a hot-melt glue gun *(Pic 3)*.

The primer surface is sanded smooth with 400 grit wet and dry paper and the plug is sprayed with an aerosol to produce the final gloss finish. The paint needs to dry thoroughly, so allow a couple of days for it to harden before giving it a final polish with 1200 grit wet and dry paper and T-Cut if it needs it *(Pic 4)*.

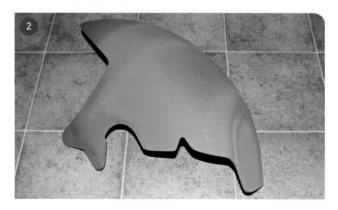

The purple colour used here was chosen to use up what was left of an aerosol can of paint which I bought to spray my wife's hat to match her dress for a family wedding. The dark colour also shows up surface imperfections well.

This hugger is basically a single curve with no returns or overhangs, so only a one-piece mould is needed. The surface can be waxed if you wish. Use two or three coats allowing each coat to fully harden before the next one is applied. Make sure no trace of wax is left on the surface

The wooden strut braces the plug and makes it easier to hold in use.

This is the surface produced after polishing the cellulose gloss finish.

Applying the PVA release agent to the plug.

before the PVA release agent is applied. Using a sponge or brush, spread a thin even coat of PVA over the whole surface and the edges of the plug *(Pic 5)*.

Allow the PVA release agent to dry fully. The plug needs to be supported clear of the bench so that it can be worked on easily *(Pic 6)*.

The hugger should be roughly measured to find its surface area. The main section is about 0.5m x 0.2m and the mounting section is about 0.2m x 0.2m so the total area is roughly 0.14m². Gelcoat coverage is 600g/m² so in theory the amount of gelcoat resin needed is 84g (0.14m x 600). So 100g or 4oz of gelcoat will give a little leeway in use. The gelcoat is weighed out into a suitable container. You should colour the gelcoat so that you can check that you are painting on an even coating.

Since the plug is finished in a dark colour the gelcoat is tinted in a light colour to make it easier to see. Light colours need a higher concentration of pigment. Usually about 7-8% is needed. For 100g of gelcoat this is about 7ml or 1½ teaspoon of pigment. Never use more than 10% pigment as it can affect the resin. Stir in the pigment thoroughly but slowly so that no air bubbles form in the resin. When the pigment is fully dispersed add the catalyst *(Pic 7)*. 2% catalyst should be fine if the temperature is correct. For 100g of resin this is 2ml or ½ teaspoon. Once

The PVA has dried to a gloss finish and the plug is supported firmly before use.

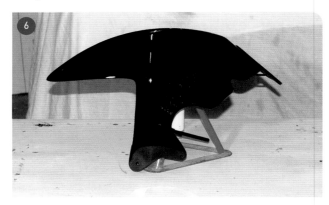

Mixing the pigment into the gelcoat resin.

again stir thoroughly but slowly. Once the catalyst is fully dispersed you have about 15–20 minutes working time which is ample for a small job like this.

The plug is given a final wipe with a Tak rag to remove dust which would otherwise be trapped permanently in the gelcoat *(Pic 8)*.

The coloured gelcoat is painted on using a 1in brush *(Pic 9)*. Try to produce an even coating about 0.5mm thick. Keep the brush well loaded and don't try to stretch the resin too thinly. It could damage the PVA release agent film.

After checking carefully for complete coverage, the plug is supported securely and the tools are cleaned out. If the sums were done correctly, there should be very little waste resin *(Pic 10)*.

After 20–30 minutes check the gelcoat by carefully touching it in an area which will not be seen on the finished panel. When ready, the gelcoat will feel sticky but no resin or colour will come off on your finger. Once the resin is set, the next step is to laminate on a layer of surface tissue. This is done to avoid areas of unsupported gelcoat if you should happen to leave an air bubble underneath the matting when you laminate on the CSM. There is no need to use one single piece of surface tissue here. Using pieces about 250mm square will make them easier to handle and to shape around the curves. Surface tissue needs about 600g/m^2 of lay-up resin to fully saturate it. This is the

same rate of coverage as the gelcoat resin, so for this job about 100g of lay-up resin is also needed. Since this is only the mould there is no point in colouring the lay-up resin. Simply weigh it out and stir in 2% (½ teaspoon) of hardener. The stirring can be more vigorous this time as tiny air bubbles no longer matter. The brush should be completely dry with no trace of any cleaning solvents remaining.

A thin coat of resin is painted over the entire plug surface *(Pic 11)*. The pieces of surface tissue are laid in place and saturated

Check the surface thoroughly for thin areas before you clean any waste resin.

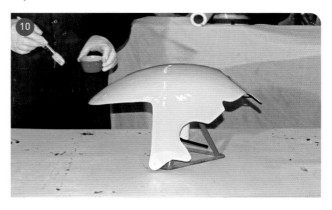

Removing traces of dust with a Tak Rag more usually used in paint shops.

Painting a thin coating of lay-up resin onto the hardened gelcoat.

Painting a layer of gelcoat resin onto the surface of the plug.

Handle the surface tissue carefully. It tears quite easily.

with resin using a gentle stippling action *(Pic 12)*. Each piece should overlap the previous one by at least 2cm and the whole surface needs to be covered with a 1-2cm overlap at the edges too *(Pic 13)*.

After making sure there are no air bubbles between the gelcoat layer and the tissue, any surplus resin is cleaned out and the brush and container are cleaned ready for the next step *(Pic 14)*.

Overlapping the tissue to ensure that the whole surface is covered.

The excess tissue can be trimmed off once the resin has hardened.

Wetting out the individual sections of CSM with lay-up resin.

When the resin has hardened the plug is ready for the final step. The mould must be rigid so that panels produced from it will have the correct shape. The curved shape of the panel will help here but three layers of 600g/m² matting will be laminated into the mould to keep it stable. To avoid excess heat build up, this will be done in two stages.

Since this is the mould, not the finished article, there is no need to accurately control the thickness of the laminate so,

Tearing the matting so that it forms easily round the curves without creasing.

Torn edges join better than cut ones.

Two layers of CSM hardening. Notice the colour change in the resin as it sets.

as with the tissue, use smaller pieces of CSM about 250mm square to build up the layers. Four pieces will be needed for each layer. The CSM should overlap the edges of the plug by 1-2cm to make sure all the edges are supported.

Two full layers of matting will weigh 300g and will need 600g of lay-up resin to saturate it if you use a roller to squeeze out air bubbles. This quantity will be no problem if you can work quickly, but for a beginner it may be better to mix up 300g of resin at a time in case it starts to set before the job is complete.

The resin is weighed out and the catalyst is stirred in. 600g of resin needs 12ml or 2½ teaspoons of catalyst for a 2% mix. As with the tissue, a paint coat of resin is applied, then each piece of CSM is laid in place and quickly saturated with resin using a stippling action *(Pic 15)*.

Make tears in the CSM to enable it to curve round the panel *(Pic 16)*. The individual pieces will mould together better if the overlapped edges are torn rather than cut *(Pic 17)*.

When the first layer is in place repeat the whole process with the second layer. The roller can be used to consolidate both layers and squeeze out any air bubbles from the final laminate. When you are happy with the laminate set it aside to harden and clean out the tools *(Pic 18)*.

Adding a foam strip which will form a stiffening ridge with the third layer of CSM.

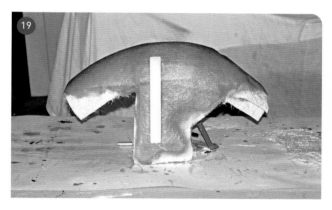

The GRP box section formed around the foam adds extra rigidity to the mould.

The third layer of CSM is added when the previous two have hardened. At this stage stiffeners can be added to the mould *(Pic 20)*. This process is described in more detail in Chapter 9.

After the final lamination is complete the mould should be left to fully harden. I would recommend that you leave finished laminations for at least 24 hours or even longer at lower temperatures. If a panel is removed from a mould or plug before it has fully cured it can distort during the final curing stages and the last thing you need is a distorted mould.

When cured, the mould needs to be separated from the plug. Before you handle the mould rub over the whole surface with 80 grit abrasive paper to remove stray strands of glassfibre. They can cut you badly once they are impregnated with resin.

To separate the laminate start at one edge or corner and work your way around the perimeter of the moulding carefully levering the more flexible plug away from the rigid mould. Use a plastic ruler or hardboard wedges to separate the two surfaces if necessary. Don't use metal objects – they will scratch the surfaces very quickly. If you did a good job with the release agents the two halves should separate easily, leaving you with a mould which only needs washing out and trimming before use. If separation is difficult, make

This is the mould removed from the plug, sanded and trimmed.

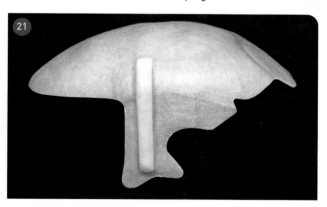

After polishing the mould surface to a high gloss it is ready for PVA to be applied.

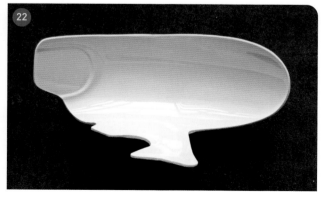

sure the mould isn't 'hooked' around the plug, then try running water between the mould and the plug to dissolve away the PVA release agent.

The original plug is no longer needed now and can be discarded or, in my case, added to the ever increasing pile of things that 'might come in handy later'. The best way to trim the mould to size is to use a cutting disc in an angle grinder. The cut edges can then be smoothed off using 80 grit abrasive paper (Pic 21).

The surface must be inspected carefully for imperfections and damage. Using PVA release agent, it is always likely that the resulting gelcoat surface may need some finishing. Dust or fluff can drop in as the PVA is drying leaving imperfections in the finish. Minor blemishes can be treated with fine wet and dry paper (1200 grit), rubbing compound and T-Cut at this stage. This is the sort of finish you are looking for before you move on (Pic 22).

When you are happy with the mould surface it is ready for

Painting coloured gelcoat resin onto the surface of the mould.

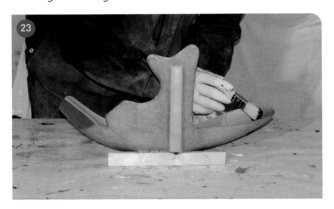

The CSM and Kevlar which will form the final hugger.

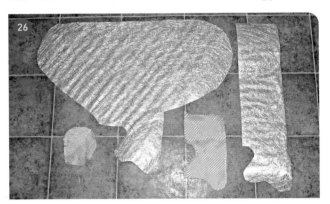

This gelcoat will end up as the outer surface of the finished hugger. Take care!

Paper patterns drawn from the plug. Useful if you want to make more than one item.

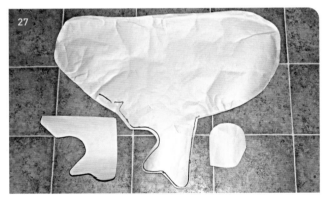

Surface tissue adds very little thickness so overlaps are no problem.

When dry the CSM will not bend to the correct contours. It creases and folds.

use. The mould surface is first treated with release wax and PVA release agent as before. To make the mould easier to use I glued on a wooden support (Pic 23).

The gelcoat resin is tinted to your chosen colour (is there any other colour but black?) and the catalyst is added. The tinted gelcoat is painted over the whole mould surface (Pic 24).

Take great care to get an even coating here as this layer will eventually form the visible outer surface of the finished item. The lay-up resin used to apply the surface tissue layer can also be coloured this time to give a more even colour and a greater depth of pigment. Once again the surface tissue can be applied in a number of small pieces as the overlaps add very little thickness (Pic 25).

The hugger in this example is a very tight fit around the wheel so the final thickness needs to be controlled carefully. This is something which is easy to do with GRP

As it wets out the CSM becomes flexible and moulds to the correct shape.

Adding the second layer of CSM which sandwiches the Kevlar and adds strength.

The single piece of matting has moulded to shape with no overlaps, folds or creases.

All the matting and fabric has been saturated with resin and lamination is complete.

Wetting out the Kevlar fabric which reinforces the mounting points.

This is the hugger exactly as it came from the mould. The finish is excellent.

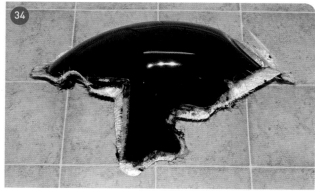

and very difficult with other materials. One layer of 600g/m² CSM will be used overall with a second layer of CSM and Kevlar fabric reinforcement at the mounting points. Each layer will be one single piece of CSM or Kevlar with no overlaps *(Pic 26)*. The original hugger was used to make paper patterns for the fabric and matting *(Pic 27)*.

This time it is probably easier to actually weigh out the matting in order to calculate the amount of resin needed. The total weight of the two layers is 200g so I need 400g of resin to fully saturate it.

You can also colour the lay-up resin for the CSM so that the component is self coloured all the way through, but until you are experienced it is probably better to leave the lay-up resin uncoloured so that you can see any air bubbles trapped in the matting. Once you are confident then go ahead and colour the lay-up resin too. The first layer of CSM is laminated into the mould. When it is dry it is difficult to form into the mould *(Pic 28)*.

As it saturates with resin the emulsion binder dissolves and the matting becomes flexible *(Pic 29)*.

When the matting was fully wetted out it formed to the mould with no creases or folds *(Pic 30)*.

The Kevlar fabric is placed in the areas needing reinforcement and wetted out with resin *(Pic 31)*.

The CSM reinforcement is positioned and saturated with resin. This piece also sandwiches the Kevlar fabric and prevents it from de-laminating *(Pic 32)*.

Finally the roller is used to fully consolidate all the layers into one unit. The job is set aside to fully cure and the tools are thoroughly cleaned out now that the job is finished *(Pic 33)*.

When the hugger is fully cured it can be separated from the mould as described previously. Don't rush this. You don't want to damage the component at this stage *(Pic 34)*.

The finished panel will need washing, trimming to size, and the edges smoothing before use. The surface should need no treatment other than a quick polish with T-Cut but could be rubbed down and sprayed with clear lacquer if required *(Pic 35)*.

This same technique can be applied to any panel no matter how large. It can also be used to reproduce panels which are damaged beyond repair. If the broken panel can be temporarily tacked together and filled to obtain a reasonable surface finish, then a mould can be made from it and a new panel can be produced. This was done to manufacture a new front panel for my Hustler Force 4 after a minor accident. Original panels were simply unobtainable *(Pic 36)*.

If the panel shape is more complex it is possible that a split mould may be needed. This is a little more involved and you will find details on how this is done in chapter 9. The next chapter will look at one method of fabricating an original item rather than copying an existing one.

Here is the finished panel trimmed and ready to fit on the bike.

My Hustler Force 4 with a new front panel made as described in the text.

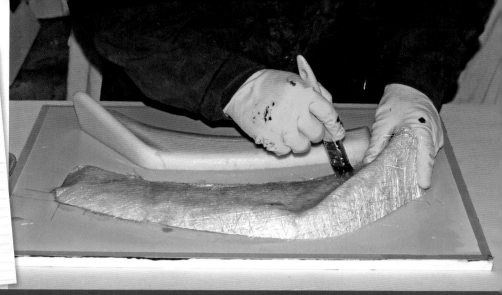

7 Making Original Components

Foam sandwich construction

No other material gives the individual user the ability to design and fabricate unique components as easily as GRP. If care is taken, complex cosmetic or structural items can be produced which would be impossible in any other material. There are a couple of techniques for doing this, depending on whether you want to make a single item or a number of copies. If the item you are making is to be a one-off, the simplest method is to skin a shaped polyurethane foam core with GRP. This is called foam sandwich construction.

Rigid Polyurethane Foam (RPU) is a denser version of the expanding foam filler available in aerosol form from DIY stores but, unlike the aerosol version, is totally resistant to attack by resin. It is available in sheets of various thicknesses and can be easily cut and sanded to shape. It has no structural strength of its own but is used as a former to be skinned with GRP. The foam is then cut away to leave the hollow GRP component ready for finishing. RPU foam is very brittle and will break if bent beyond a very gentle curve, but

A cardboard endplate temporarily glued in place to check the fit.

Marking the panel shape on cardboard to form a template.

A sheet of 25mm thick polyurethane foam.

there is a version known as Scoreboard which has grooves machined in it to allow a small amount of flexibility.

To demonstrate fabrication by this method I thought I would make a pair of corner splitters for my wife's car, a Chevrolet Matiz.

The contours of the bodywork are marked out onto a cardboard template [Pic 1].

The cardboard is cut and glued temporarily with a hot glue gun to get an idea of how it may look on the car [Pic 2].

25mm thick foam is convenient to use and can be glued together with resin or hot glue to form thicker blocks. The foam cuts easily with a hacksaw blade or even a sharp kitchen knife. The dust produced is harmful, so wear a face mask and eye protection when you are cutting or sanding the foam [Pic 3].

The templates are used to mark out the foam ready for cutting [Pic 4]. A Stanley knife blade is ideal for making curved cuts in the foam. Don't try to cut the whole depth of the foam in one go. Make a shallow cut first then use it as a guide to cut through the foam in two or three passes [Pic 5].

For straight cuts a long blade is better. I have an old kitchen knife which works well with this foam. There are two horizontal sections and two endplates to cut out [Pic 6].

Marking the shape of the splitter on the foam.

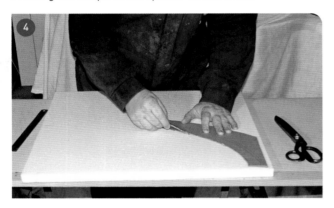

Making the initial cut in the foam using a Stanley knife blade.

The main splitter sections cut from the foam.

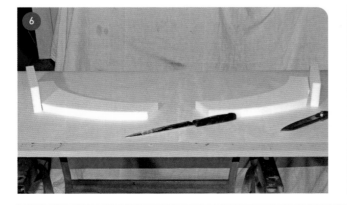

Cutting the correct angle for the splitter end plates.

Checking the fit of the endplates.

Applying the hot melt glue.

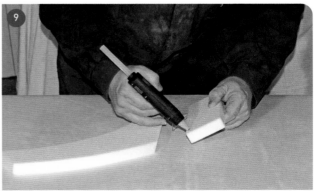

The end plates will be mounted at an angle so the ends of the splitter are cut using a template to get the angle correct [Pic 7].

The fit of the endplates needs to checked before being glued in place. If you try to pull the foam apart once it has been glued it will crack or break [Pic 8].

Hot melt glue is ideal for gluing the foam but try to keep the glue away from areas which will need to be sanded. The glue is flexible and does not sand very well. The foam is an excellent heat insulator so the glue cools very slowly. You may need to hold the parts in place for longer than normal [Pic 9].

To avoid the sharp corner where the foam blocks meet, a foam fillet has been glued in place [Pic 10]. It will be sanded to a smooth curve when the splitter is shaped.

Initial shaping can be done with a sharp knife. A long blade will help to produce straighter cuts [Pic 11]. Carve the shape

The foam formers ready for initial shaping.

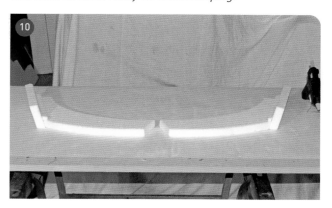

An old kitchen knife is used to carve the foam.

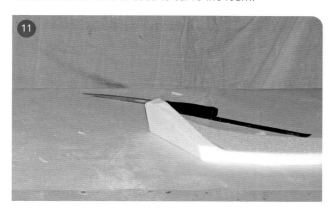

Carefully shaping the foam with 80 grit abrasive paper on a sanding block.

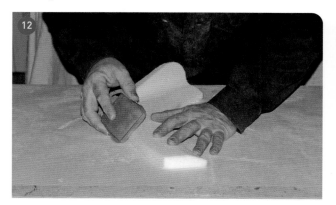

Sanding a smooth internal curve with abrasive paper wrapped round a tube.

The final foam shapes have large radius curves to allow the CSM to follow them without lifting.

Painting on a coat of catalysed lay-up resin.

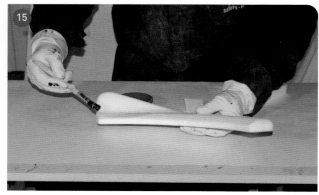

roughly, then use 80 and 120 grit abrasive papers to produce the final shapes. Don't be too worried about the surface finish as all the foam will be cut away once the GRP skin has hardened *(Pics 12 & 13)*.

Try to avoid sharp corners and edges in the design *(Pic 14)*. CSM will not bend around curves tighter than about 6mm radius. It lifts off the former or mould leaving bubbles and voids.

The foam is quite fragile where it is thinner in section. A coating of lay-up resin will make it more rigid and support it when you laminate onto it *(Pics 15 & 16)*.

The foam shapes coated with resin for rigidity.

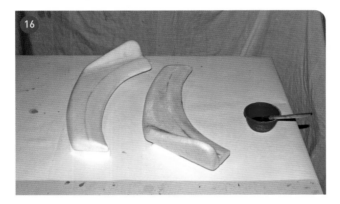

The foam formers glued to a backing board for rigidity.

Painting a coat of resin onto the formers before laminating on the CSM.

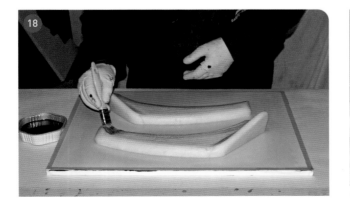

To make it easier to handle and to help keep it in shape whilst it is being skinned, the foam core needs to be temporarily mounted on a flat rigid surface. Hot glue is perfect for this. I usually use another piece of foam or a piece of melamine faced board. If you use melamine board paint on a coating of PVA release agent so that the CSM does not stick to it *(Pic 17)*.

Once the foam is mounted firmly it can be skinned with GRP. Paint a thin layer of catalysed lay-up resin onto the foam former *(Pic 18)*.

Lining up the CSM. When wetted out the matting will form to the correct shape.

Holding the matting in place until it is saturated with resin.

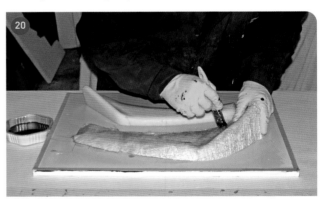

Tearing the matting so that it bends round the tight curve.

The GRP skin will form the outer surface of the final component so, to minimise filling and sanding, the CSM finish needs to be as smooth as possible. Any overlaps in the matting will leave steps or raised areas which will need to be sanded smooth. Try to cut the matting so as to produce the minimum number of areas of overlap. Ideally one single piece of CSM should cover the whole shape as shown in this example (Pic 19).

The CSM is weighed so that the correct amount of resin can be mixed up. There is no point in colouring this resin as the surface will need filling and painting later anyway.

The matting must be fully saturated with resin and care needs to be taken to remove any air bubbles below the matting. Bubbles will cause a lump in the matting which will need to be sanded smooth (Pic 20).

The matting forms round the curved shapes well but needs tearing in the tighter areas (Pic 21).

These particular components need only one layer of CSM at this stage but larger items may need a couple of layers to keep them rigid. A layer of surface tissue could also be added here to reduce the amount of smoothing and filling needed later (Pic 22).

When you are satisfied that the CSM is fully wetted out, leave the laminate to cure and clean up the tools before the resin sets (Pic 23).

When the GRP has fully cured, remove any loose strands with abrasive paper and lift the moulding away from the base board. Carefully cut away the foam from the inside and use 80 grit abrasive paper to remove any traces of foam stuck to the inside of the GRP.

If more layers are needed for strength they can be added to the inside or the outside of the component depending on where clearance is more important. In this case a second layer of matting was laminated onto the inside of each moulding (Pic 24).

The disadvantage of this method of construction is the poor

Removing air bubbles by stippling the resin into the matting.

The foam formers completely skinned with GRP.

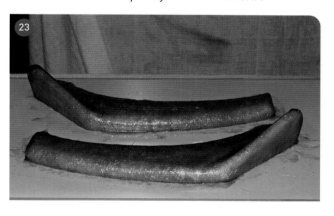

After trimming the mouldings a second layer of matting is laminated inside the first.

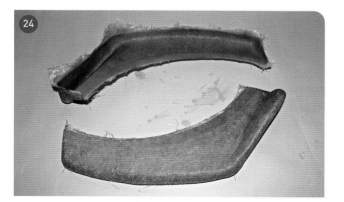

The entire outer surface is covered with a layer of body filler.

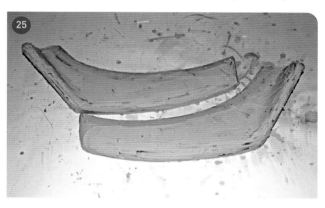

After smoothing the filler with abrasive paper very little remains in the low spots.

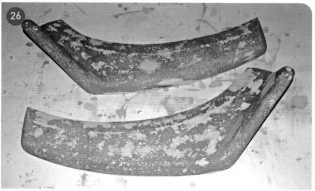

surface finish obtained. It will be rough and uneven and will need a lot of work with filler and abrasives to produce a smooth surface ready for painting. Use 80 grit abrasive paper to remove the high spots on the glassfibre before moving on to body filler. Don't attempt to do all the filling in one stage. Start by covering the moulding in a layer of filler 0.5-1mm thick (Pic 25).

When it hardens, smooth the filler with 80 grit abrasive paper. Almost all the filler should be removed, apart from what remains in the low spots on the moulding (Pic 26).

Inspect the surface carefully. There will still be some small imperfections left behind. These will need a second, much smaller, application of filler which can be rubbed down when set. I usually plan on using three coats of filler to obtain a smooth surface. I smooth the third layer with 120 grit abrasive paper in preparation for rubbing down with 400 grit wet and dry paper and priming the surface. There is no gelcoat surface using this method of fabrication so when primed the finish will be covered in pinholes caused by tiny air bubbles trapped in the CSM (Pic 27).

The primed surface. Notice all the pinholes.

The splitters sprayed with a colour matched aerosol.

Two coats of spray putty followed by knifing stopper.

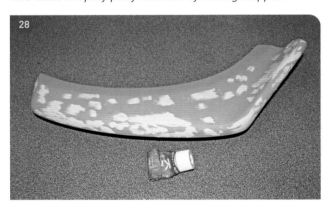

The finished splitters mounted on the car.

One splitter showing the paint guide coat and the other flatted for spraying.

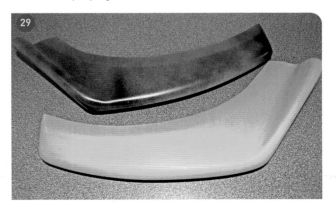

The angle of the endplate matches the angle of the wheel arch edge.

Aerosol spray putty (filler primer) may fill them or you may have to use knifing putty (stopper) *(Pic 28)*.

Hopefully when the stopper is rubbed down the surface should be smooth and ready to spray with the chosen colour. In this case a couple more coats of spray putty were needed. A dusting of a contrasting colour is sprayed on to act as a guide coat then, using 600 grit wet and dry paper, the surface is wet flatted until the entire guide coat is removed. This ensures that the final surface is perfectly flat and smooth *(Pic 29)*.

The colour coat is sprayed onto this prepared surface and the components are finally ready to fit *(Pic 30)*.

The finished splitters can be fitted with screws, silicone sealant or a polyurethane adhesive *(Pics 31 & 32)*.

Only painted components can be produced by this method due to the amount of surface finishing needed. If the component is required to have a self-coloured gloss gelcoat finish or a carbon fibre weave finish then it would have to be laminated in a well prepared mould as described previously. The next chapter describes the production of an original item from a plug and mould.

8 Making Original Components

Plugs and moulds

If you want to produce a GRP component with a professional looking self-coloured gelcoat finish or if you want a clear gelcoat with a visible carbon fibre or Kevlar weave, then your only option is to laminate the component in a high quality female mould. This is also the technique to use if you want to produce a number of copies of your item. Since we are dealing with unique components of your own design, you will first have to make your own mould. The mould, in turn, needs to be taken from a 'plug' which must be an exact replica of the item you are trying to make. This probably sounds like a lot of hard work and actually it is. At each stage the shape and surface finish must be as near perfect as possible, since the final component will be a copy of the plug but will also reproduce any surface imperfections picked up along the way. The only good news here is that the plug can be made from materials which can be cut and worked easily or even

from objects which are already the correct shape. I needed a compact washer reservoir for my car so I made this container from two identical GRP halves bonded together. The plug used to make the mould was the bottom of a polythene water carrier *(Pic 1)*.

This time I am going to demonstrate the procedure by making a typical teardrop bonnet bulge. These can come in very handy if you are having minor clearance problems between the bonnet and, for example, an air filter or oil filler neck.

The first step is to produce the plug (or buck as it is sometimes known) from which you can take a mould. The plug has to be a perfect copy of the bulge you are trying to make. It doesn't matter what it is made from so it makes sense to choose materials which are easy to work with. Wood can certainly be used but I would suggest you consider Balsa rather than Teak. Since it is designed for the job, rigid polyurethane foam makes a good choice but this time it will

A windscreen washer bottle made from two identical halves taken from a mould made around a polythene water carrier.

A typical teardrop shape drawn out as a pattern for the plug.

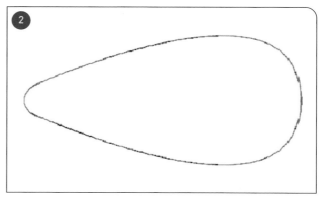

need to be coated in a material which can be sanded to a fine finish and painted.

A paper pattern is a good idea to ensure that you get the basic shape right. I drew this one using the 'Paint' computer program but if you have an artistic bent you can just draw it freehand (Pic 2).

The pattern is used to mark out the foam which is then cut roughly to shape (Pics 3 and 4).

The foam cuts easily and a sharp knife produces less dust than a saw blade. It is also easier to get vertical cuts with a knife (Pic 5).

As before, 80 and 120 grit abrasive papers are used to shape the foam. It sands very quickly and it is easy to remove too much if you are not careful. Wrapping the sandpaper round a block will help to control the process and also avoids grooves in the foam caused by your fingers behind the abrasive (Pic 6).

A small piece of 1in thick foam to produce the plug.

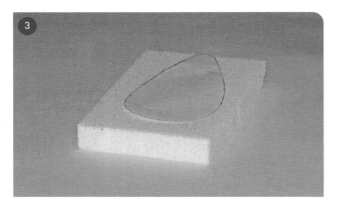

Marking out the shape of the bulge on the foam.

Using a sharp knife to roughly trim the foam to shape.

A sanding block will help to avoid grooves caused by finger pressure.

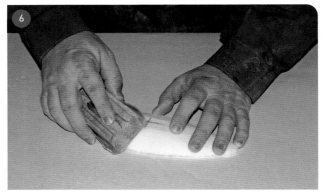

Wrapping the sandpaper around a large tube will help to form concave curves.

For final shaping and moulding the foam needs to be mounted on a rigid backing.

If you are forming a shape which has concave curves, the abrasive can be wrapped around a piece of tubing or a suitably sized socket (Pic 7).

As the edges of the shape become thinner it needs to be glued to a baseboard for support (Pic 8). Hot melt glue is perfect for this. Once the shape is fully supported the final shape can be sanded using 120 or 220 grit paper (Pic 9).

The final shaping is done carefully as the foam sands very quickly.

The filler has been thinned slightly with water so that it can be brushed on.

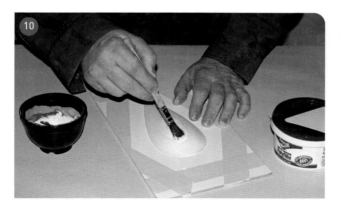

This first layer will need sanding down when dry and further layers may be needed before a smooth shape is achieved.

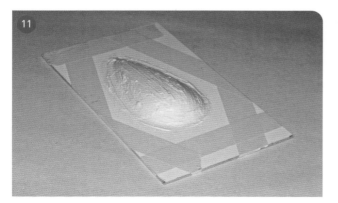

The foam then needs to be coated with a material which can be sanded smooth and painted to produce a gloss finish. A couple of coats of lay-up or gelcoat resin will work but they do not sand very easily. Body filler can certainly be used but the household fillers such as Tetrion or Polyfilla are even easier to sand and will be fine for a temporary job like this. Thin the filler slightly with water and spread a thin layer over

The foam and filler plug shaped, smoothed and ready for primer.

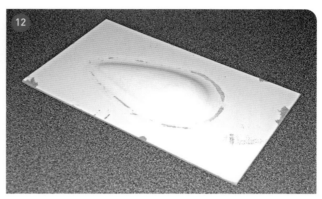

The filler primer after wet flatting with 1200 grit paper. No gloss coat will be needed in this case.

Painting the tinted gelcoat onto the prepared plug surface. The masking tape simply marks out the important area of the item.

the foam. I find it easier to use a brush once it has been thinned. Allow the first coat to harden (Pic 10).

Don't worry too much about the surface finish at this stage. It will need to be sanded down and it is likely that further coats of filler will be needed before the final finish is obtained (Pic 11).

Smooth the dry filler with 120 grit paper. If you break through the layer of filler you will need to add some more and start again. When you have the shape you need you can smooth it with 220 grit paper ready for the primer (Pic 12).

If you are using wood as a former you can probably by-pass the filler stage as the primer has enough build to fill the grain of the wood. Spray on three or four coats of primer and let it harden completely. Wet sand the primer with 400 grit wet and dry paper until it is smooth. Check the surface for imperfections. If there are any low areas they can be filled with spray putty or knifing stopper and rubbed down again (Pic 13). When you are satisfied with the surface you can spray it with two or three coats of cellulose gloss paint. The colour is not important but the surface finish is.

Leave it to harden for three or four days before polishing it to a high gloss with T-Cut or similar. Once the plug is ready to use, the hard work is over. The plug is coated with PVA release agent then layers of gelcoat, surface tissue and CSM are laminated over the plug in the usual way and allowed to harden (Pic 14).

When the mould and plug have been separated, the plug can be discarded. If polyurethane foam is used as a base the plug often breaks up anyway as it is removed from the mould. The mould itself can be trimmed and the mould surface can be prepared to produce the final bulge (Pic 15).

Check the surface of the mould carefully for imperfections. If necessary the surface can be wet sanded with 1200 grit

The mould removed from the plug. The brittle foam plug cracked during the separation but is no longer needed .

Carefully pushing the carbon fibre fabric into the mould so that the weave pattern is not distorted.

The mould polished up and treated with PVA release agent.

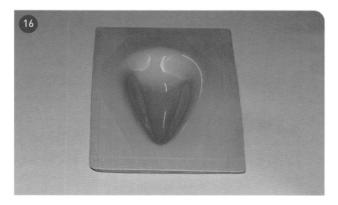

Painting on a thin even coating of clear gelcoat resin.

The carbon fibre layer wetted out with lay-up resin.

wet & dry paper and polished with T-Cut. Believe it or not, you are almost there. Once the mould is prepared with a coating of PVA release agent it is ready to use *(Pic 16)*.

This time we will try for a carbon fibre finish. The gelcoat resin needs to be transparent so no pigment is added. Carefully paint on a thin even coating and allow it to set *(Pic 17)*.

If the gelcoat is uneven it will spoil the appearance of the carbon fibre underneath. No surface tissue layer is used since the carbon fibre weave needs to be visible through the surface. The carbon fibre fabric has been cut so that the weave pattern lines up along the axis of the bulge, but that is purely my choice. It depends what weave pattern you are using.

The carbon cloth is carefully laminated onto the clear gelcoat. Don't distort the weave as you stipple on the resin but make sure no air bubbles are trapped under the cloth. Either will spoil the appearance of the finished bulge *(Pic 18)*. Use just enough resin to wet out the fabric. Try not to let free resin build up in the mould *(Pic 19)*.

Carbon fibre cloth can have quite an open weave and light can pass through it, so when this layer has hardened the carbon fibre needs to be backed up with one layer of black tinted CSM to make the moulding opaque *(Pic 20)*.

When this final layer has fully hardened the finished bulge can be separated from the mould and trimmed to suit *(Pics 21 and 22)*.

Once you have the mould you can produce as many replicas of the bulge as you need. Many years ago I owned a Mini Marcos. As standard they have two small teardrop bulges in the bonnet to provide clearance for the twin SU carburettors fitted to performance versions of the A series engine. I fitted a large single carburettor to my car and needed additional clearance for this set up. I took a mould from one of the original bulges and used it to produce the third central bulge you see on my car *(Pic 23)*.

I still have this mould and, over the years, I have made numerous copies of the bulge for owners and builders of a wide variety of cars.

Up to this point we have used simple one piece moulds. The next chapter deals with the production of the multi piece moulds needed for components with a more complex shape.

Laminating in a single layer of CSM with black resin to make the moulding opaque.

The three stages in the fabrication of an original component. The plug, the mould and the final item.

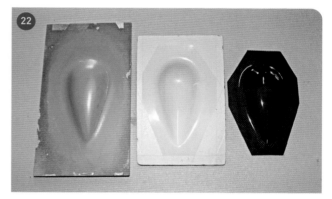

The completed bulge. This finish is exactly as it came from the mould. Notice how the weave of the fabric lines up with the axis of the bulge.

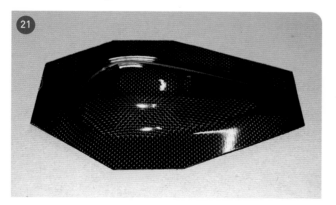

Mini Marcos with additional central bonnet bulge.

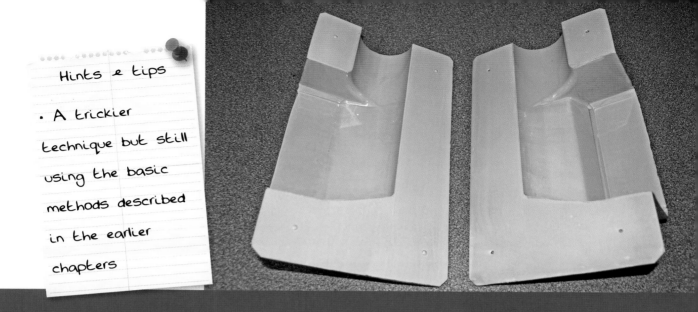

9 Advanced Techniques - Part 1

Split moulds

So far the moulds we have made have been taken from simple convex shapes with no rebates or returns. The moulds have lifted away from the plug easily *(Pic 1)*.

If the shape is more complex, however, it may be that a one piece mould will not work. The mould may hook around the plug and be impossible to remove *(Pic 2)*.

In these cases we have to produce a split mould. This is made in separate sections for easy removal from the plug. It is clamped or bolted together to mould the required item in one piece *(Pic 3)*.

For a large or complex shape a multi piece mould may be needed. The removable front end which I made for my racer needed a four piece split mould *(Pic 4)*.

To illustrate the use of split moulds I will fabricate a GRP air box intended to form part of a cold air induction system for my GTM. The plug for the air box has been shaped from polyurethane foam, body filler and a GRP tube made in a

mould taken from a section of plastic drainpipe. You could actually use the drainpipe itself if you wanted *(Pic 5)*.

This mould will not separate from the plug. It will snag in the concave areas indicated.

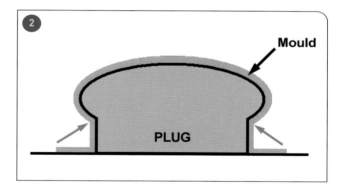

A two piece mould split as shown will separate easily from the plug but can be re-assembled easily for use.

A mould formed round a plug of this basic shape will lift off easily.

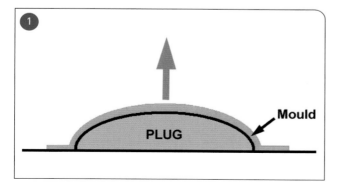

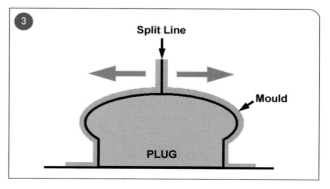

As always, the surface finish of the plug is vital, so a lot of time and effort goes into its preparation. The plug is primed with an aerosol primer, sprayed with two coats of filler/primer and any pin holes filled with stopper. The stopper is smoothed and two further coats of filler primer are sprayed on. Final flatting was done with 1200 grit wet and dry paper producing a surface which is smooth enough to use with no gloss top coat *(Pic 6)*.

The mould will be made in two halves with flanges enabling the halves to be clamped or bolted together. To produce the first half of the mould, temporary dividers need to be fixed to the plug along the proposed split line. These dividing flanges need to be a tight fit around the plug, so a paper pattern is made first *(Pic 7)*.

Using the paper patterns the dividers are carefully cut from thin GRP sheet *(Pic 8)*. Hardboard works well too.

The dividers need to be temporarily attached to the plug. Hot melt glue may damage the paint so I am using plasticine.

This mould is in four sections, bolted together and supported by wooden batons for rigidity.

Pieces of paper are used to make accurate patterns for the flange dividers.

This is the foam, GRP and filler plug sanded to shape.

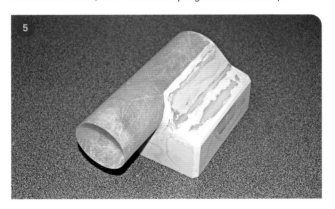

This is an actual divider cut from thin GRP sheet.

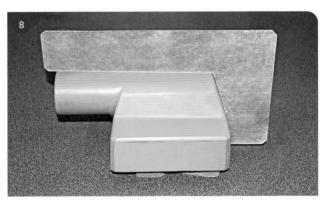

The plug has been primed, filled, re-primed and wet sanded with 1200 grit paper.

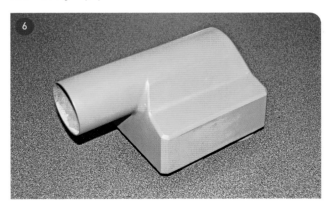

The plasticine fills the gap between the dividers and the plug, preventing resin from leaking through.

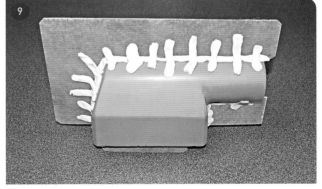

If it is warmed with a hair dryer or on a radiator it becomes soft and sticky but hardens again when it cools. It must be handled carefully when it cools down as it is not particularly sticky when cold. Excess plasticine can be scraped away using a plastic scraper to avoid scratching the paint *(Pic 9)*.

The oil from the plasticine must be removed from the surface of the plug as it will prevent the PVA release agent from spreading correctly. White Spirit will clean excess plasticine and oil from the plug easily *(Pic 10)*.

The finished plug ready for the release agent and GRP.

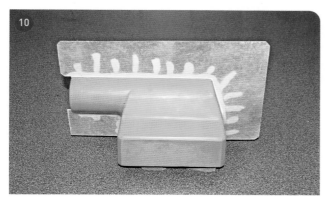

The gelcoat is painted on very gently to avoid dislodging the dividers. The same care needs to be taken with the tissue coat too.

This diagram shows how the layers of CSM must be laminated to form a sharp corner.

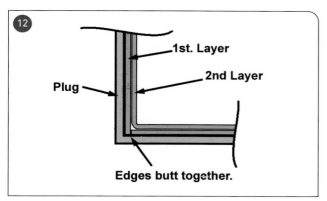

The working side of the plug and dividing flanges are treated with PVA release agent and are ready for use. The gelcoat and surface tissue must be applied carefully to avoid cracking the flanges away from the plug *(Pic 11)*.

Once the tissue layer has hardened the structure will be less fragile and the layers of CSM can be laminated on in the normal way.

The CSM will not bend round the sharp internal corners on the plug where the dividers join the main structure. It will lift away from the surface leaving voids. To avoid this the first layer of CSM is made up of narrow strips of matting with cut edges. The edges of the matting are laminated into the sharp corners so that the edges butt together. The first layer is allowed to harden before further layers are added. These layers will lift away from the corner forming a void but the gelcoat and tissue will still be well supported by the first CSM layer *(Pic 12)*. A similar technique is used to form sharp external corners too.

Strips of CSM 75mm wide are used in the first layer. The cut edges are carefully laminated into the corners *(Pic 13)*.

The pieces of CSM must butt together with no gaps or overlaps *(Pic 14)*.

Using this technique the whole of the plug is covered with a single layer of CSM which is then allowed to set *(Pic 15)*.

The cut edge of the CSM is carefully laminated into the corner.

Butting the second piece of CSM up to the first to form the sharp corner.

When this layer has hardened the subsequent layers can be laminated on in the normal way. The small size and complex shape of this plug means that three layers should be fine (Pic 16).

Once the lamination is fully hardened the plasticine can be removed and the dividers can be separated from the mould. The flanges are now formed as an integral part of the

mould. They need to be trimmed and cleaned up to remove traces of plasticine and release agent (Pic 17).

Four or five small countersinks are made in the flange with a 6mm drill. When the second half of the mould is laminated, gelcoat resin will flow into these holes and set to form small pimples on the matching flange. These holes and pimples

Laminating the first layer of CSM with cut edges forming the sharp corners on the plug.

Drilling some small depressions in the flange so that they will form locating points when the second half of the mould is laminated onto the plug.

One side of the split mould is now completed and fully hardened.

These are the two halves of the mould trimmed and cleaned ready for use.

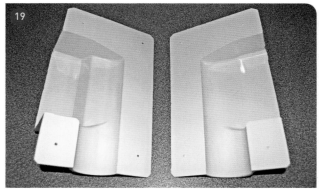

The dividers have been removed to show the flanges which have been formed as part of the mould

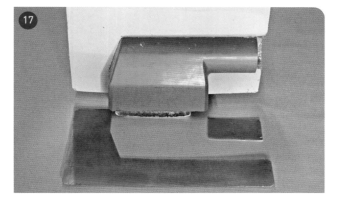

The locating dimples (arrowed right) have formed in the countersunk holes (left) drilled before the second half of the mould was laminated.

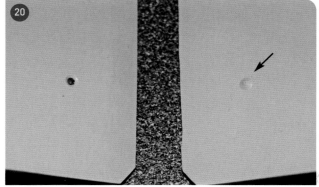

will locate the two halves of the mould exactly when they are clamped together for use *(Pic 18)*.

The surfaces are now ready to be treated with PVA release agent followed by layers of gelcoat, tissue and CSM laminated onto the plug to form the second half of the split mould.

Once the second half of the mould has fully cured the two halves can be separated from the plug. With a complex shape

Gelcoat damage caused when the mould was separated from the plug.

The mould halves are treated with PVA release agent. The flanges are also treated in case any resin leaks between them.

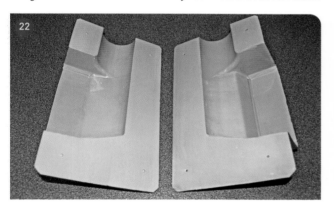

If you get everything lined up correctly, the join line should be almost invisible.

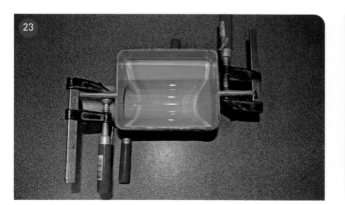

like this it is unlikely that the plug, made from brittle polyurethane foam, will survive without breaking but this is not important as the plug is no longer needed anyway. The two halves of the mould can be trimmed, washed and inspected for damage. Any imperfections can be repaired at this stage and polished out if required *(Pic 19)*.

The locating pips and holes should have formed on the two halves of the mould and will assist in lining up the halves when they are clamped together *(Pic 20)*.

During the separation of the moulds from the plug an area of gelcoat resin cracked away from the sharp edge at the mould joining face *(Pic 21)*.

This damage could be permanently repaired with body filler sanded to a smooth finish but a quicker alternative is to wait until the moulds are clamped together then temporarily fill any holes or cracks with plasticine. Resin will not stick to plasticine and it will clean off the finished moulding easily with white spirit.

The polished moulds are given a coating of PVA release agent. You can do this when the two halves are clamped together if you wish but this shape is quite complex and it would be easy to miss an area with the PVA, so I have coated the two halves separately *(Pic 22)*.

When the PVA has dried the two halves can be clamped

This area of missing gelcoat needs to be repaired before the mould is used.

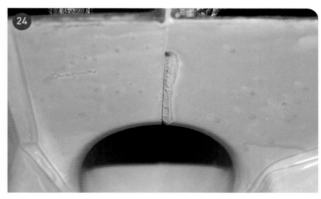

Plasticine has been used to fill the crack and the release agent has been re-touched.

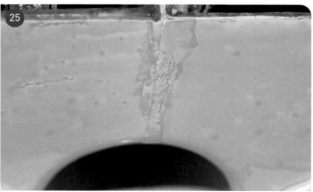

together. Line them up carefully. Any misalignment at this stage will cause a lot of work later on when the finished item needs to be repaired [Pic 23].

Before this mould is used the damaged gelcoat needs to be repaired otherwise it will appear as a major blemish on the completed air box [Pic 24].

As mentioned earlier, the damage will be temporarily repaired with plasticine. While you have the plasticine handy it is worth checking the whole joint line in the mould in case any other small gaps need to be filled. When the plasticine has been smoothed down any damage to the PVA release agent can be re-touched [Pic 25].

At this stage the mould is ready to use. A layer of gelcoat is painted into the mould first. The mould is an awkward shape so extra care is needed to make sure an even coating is obtained [Pic 26].

This particular lamination was being done on a day when the outside temperature was about -7°C. My fan heater was not up to the job of heating the whole garage to a suitable temperature and I was working to a deadline so I needed to heat a smaller volume instead. The moulding was placed inside a large cardboard box and the heater was placed facing the opening to maintain a warm environment inside the box. This should really only be considered for emergencies, as it is very easy to overheat the moulding causing the gelcoat to separate from the mould or causing a dangerous heat build up in a CSM laminate. Start with the heater well away from the box and monitor the temperature inside the box constantly. It should feel barely warm. If the mouldings themselves start to heat up they should be removed from the heated area [Pic 27].

The gelcoat is backed up with a layer of surface tissue, which is allowed to harden, and then the CSM is laminated into the mould. The shape of the mould makes it impossible to use a roller to consolidate the matting, so great care must be taken with the brush to make sure that the matting is fully wetted out and forced into all the corners and curves in the mould [Pic 28].

As always, the moulding is left to fully cure before being removed from the mould. The two halves of the mould are carefully unclamped and peeled away from the workpiece.

The edges are trimmed and the moulding is washed to remove dust and traces of PVA release agent. The final result was good, with only a faint line showing where the split in the mould had been. This could be rubbed down and polished out if required [Pic 29].

Producing a component from a multi-piece mould is time consuming but not really any more difficult than producing

Carefully heating a small space to allow the resin to set or cure.

A roller cannot be used in this case so the matting has to be wetted out using just the brush. Notice how my overalls have picked up so much resin that they are now difficult to distinguish from the mould and workpiece.

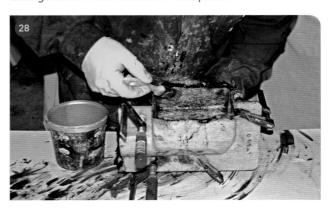

The finished air box just as it came from the mould. The surface is good and the mould split line is barely visible.

Painting the black tinted gelcoat into the mould.

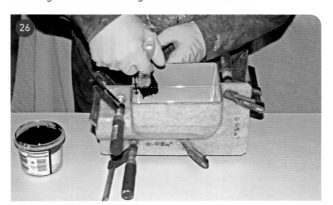

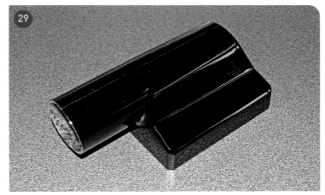

one from a single piece mould. Each section of the mould requires its own laminating sequence and you have to plan and produce the dividers for the separate mould sections but the process is still well within the scope of the amateur builder, as I have shown here.

So far, the components produced have been relatively small and their shape has provided sufficient rigidity. As panels get bigger and flatter this no longer applies. The next chapter looks at ways of adding rigidity to GRP panels.

10 Advanced Techniques - Part 2
Adding stiffness without weight

A 1mm thick steel sheet is much stiffer than a 1mm thick sheet of GRP. If the steel sheet is then pressed into a curved shape, such as a car door or bonnet, the action of bending the steel introduces tension which adds further stiffness to the panel. A curved GRP panel will be more rigid than a flat one due to the extra depth introduced by the curve, but there is no tensioning effect equivalent to that produced by bending steel. GRP panels can be made stiffer by making them thicker. A GRP panel typically needs to be two or three times thicker than a steel panel to approach the same stiffness.

This extra thickness obviously introduces a weight penalty and can also cause fitting problems if the GRP panel is to be a direct replacement for a steel one. Fortunately, as we have seen, it is possible to control and vary the thickness of a GRP moulding by varying the number of layers or the thickness of the CSM used in the moulding. We could, for example, make the centre of a panel thicker for rigidity but leave the perimeter thinner so that it will fit correctly against a door seal or a gutter section. We could use Coremat sandwiched between layers of CSM to add thickness and rigidity to specific areas. Coremat is designed to absorb less resin than CSM so although there is some weight penalty, it is not as great as using CSM alone to add the extra thickness. My personal choice is to add stiffness without weight by forming ribs and box sections on the panel. The stiffening ribs can be added after the panel is completed or formed as an integral part of the moulding process. If you open the bonnet of any production car you will see stiffening ribs attached, normally by bonding, to the underside of the panel. These ribs can be duplicated on a GRP panel but can actually be made as part of the panel rather than being added on later (Pic 1).

The material used to form the rib is not important since the strength comes from the glassfibre box section it produces, not from the material itself. I have heard of rolled-up newspaper being used successfully and I have, in the past, used shaped wooden sections in areas where there was no possibility of water contact (Pic 2).

If wood gets wet it swells and can split or de-laminate the GRP so if you choose to use wood as a former, balsa wood is the most suitable. I now prefer to use the materials specifically designed for the purpose, namely paper rope or polyurethane foam. The paper rope, which is available in various sizes, has a 'D' shaped cross section and a wire stiffener down the centre (Pic 3).

It can be bent to shape and glued onto a GRP panel with a hot melt glue gun then covered with glassfibre. The resulting box section adds strength out of all proportion to its weight

The small panel on the left is much more rigid than the one on the right but weighs only 5g more.

and the paper rope will not damage the lamination should water enter the stiffener at a later date. Polyurethane foam can be used in the same way and is more versatile since the width or height of the stiffening ribs can be varied when the foam is cut to size *(Pic 4)*.

Some thought needs to be put into the way the bracing is arranged. In particular, you need to make sure that there is sufficient clearance underneath the panel. It would be a shame to laminate a beautiful lightweight bonnet and then find that the stiffening ribs foul the air filter or master cylinders. Common layouts would be a perimeter frame or simple diagonal bracing *(Pic 5)*.

Too much foam material can actually reduce strength by

Half round wooden dowel and polyurethane foam used to form stiffening ribs on a GRP floor panel.

Generally the diagonal bracing will add more rigidity, particularly if the panel already has a flange or return around the edge.

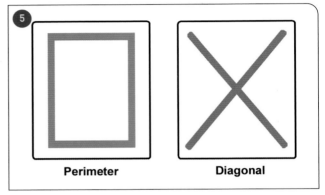

The paper rope is loosely stitched to bind it together and has thin steel wire down the centre so that it will hold a shape when bent.

The design on the right is better as it allows plenty of contact between layers of CSM.

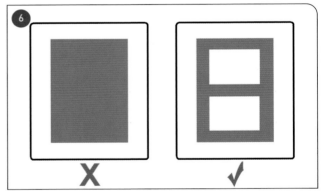

This is a mudguard mould which has been stiffened by ribs formed over polyurethane foam strips. The foam is glued onto the curved panel in small sections.

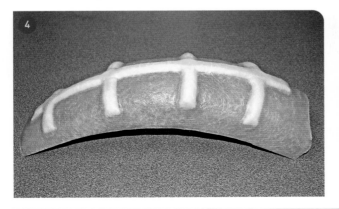

This is the mould after washing. It needs checking for defects, repairing if necessary and polishing before use.

preventing layers of CSM from bonding together. Strengthening ribs are better than large areas of foam (Pic 6).

To demonstrate the use of stiffeners I will laminate a lightweight GRP boot lid. Over the years I have accumulated many strange objects, one of which is a fairly crude mould for an Austin Healey 3000 competition type boot lid. It is the type which has an extra bulge for a second spare wheel. To show what is possible with GRP I intend to make the moulding very light using gelcoat, tissue and only two layers of CSM. To ensure adequate panel stiffness I will laminate stiffening ribs into the moulding incorporating them into the second CSM layer.

The mould has stood unused for a few years and needs to be renovated and re-polished with rubbing compound and T-Cut (Pic 7).

It is then treated with PVA release agent in the usual way. The grey tinted gelcoat is painted on and, when set, backed up by a layer of surface tissue wetted out with matching grey tinted resin (Pic 8).

One full layer of 600g/m² CSM is applied along with Kevlar patches and an extra thickness of CSM at the hinge and lock mounting points. This layer is allowed to harden but not fully cure. The second layer will bond better if the first layer is still

'green'. Do not remove the panel from the mould at this stage or it may distort when the stiffening is added. The foam can now be cut to shape to produce the formers for the stiffening ribs (Pic 9).

The formers are glued into position and shaped so that the second layer of CSM will drape over them. These thin strips

Using a hot melt glue gun, the strips are glued into position. They are positioned to give stiffness in the larger unsupported areas.

The corners have been sanded away to produce a 'D' section so that the CSM will drape over them.

This is quite a large area (0.75m2) so you need to work fairly quickly or the gelcoat resin may begin to set in the pot.

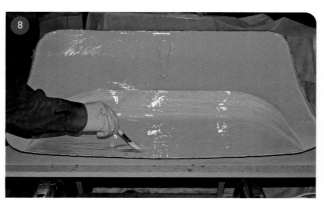

This is the finished boot lid with Kevlar reinforcement for the hinges and handle, and stiffening ribs in the unsupported areas.

The 25mm thick polyurethane foam is cut into strips about 6-8mm thick.

will bend through gentle curves without breaking (Pic 10).

Sharp corners will cause the matting to separate from the former, so edges are rounded and smoothed (Pic 11).

The formers should be at least 2cm apart so that the matting can bond fully to the material between them and for the same reason they should not be too close to the edge of the panel either. The second layer of CSM is now laminated over the foam and the GRP panel. The matting is stippled and rolled into any folds and corners (Pic 12).

When the lamination is complete, the panel is allowed to fully harden and cure before it is removed from the mould. It can be trimmed and finished in the usual way. (Pic 13)

The panel, at less than 4kg, is as light as a normal two layer lamination but is significantly more rigid as a result of the built in stiffening ribs (Pic 14).

In the past, the need to stiffen specific areas of glassfibre mouldings has not always been appreciated. There have been examples of cars where panels would sag after a period of use or where the roof was so flexible that, at high speed, it would pull away from the top of the windscreen. Hopefully, in this chapter, I have shown you how to plan and fabricate panels which can be made as rigid as you require without any weight penalty whatsoever.

At this point I feel I have described and demonstrated most of the techniques you will need and most of the materials you are likely to come across when fabricating components for automotive use. The following chapters will deal with the methods commonly used to bond or fix panels to vehicles and to repair damaged gelcoat finishes and GRP panels.

This is the completed boot lid after trimming and washing to remove release agent and dust.

The pronounced bulge in this version of the big Healey boot lid is to allow two spare wheels to be stacked together in the boot.

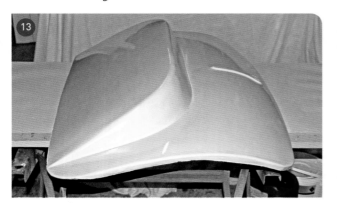

11 Advanced Techniques - Part 3
Fasteners and fixings

Once you have produced your GRP panel, bulge, scoop or spoiler you have the problem of fixing it to the vehicle. Many of the fastening systems designed to work with metal panels are less successful when used in GRP, so it makes sense to think about the fastening system for the panel during the design stage. There are quite a few possibilities.

Bonding with glassfibre

If you are trying to permanently join two GRP panels then bonding them together with resin and CSM is probably the simplest solution. The panels and the bonding material will flex at the same rate and there should be no cracking problems. I filled the sunroof panel in my car with a piece of GRP sheet bonded in using CSM strips and resin. The CSM overlaps both panels by 50-75mm to give sufficient bonding area. I also reinforced the area with stiffening ribs *(Pic 1)*.

To successfully bond panels together, the area where the CSM will be applied needs to be roughened to provide a good key. A sanding disc or a twist knot wire brush in an angle grinder will do a good job on larger areas but 80 grit abrasive paper and hard work will handle smaller areas. The panels need to be held firmly in place while the CSM is being wetted out with resin. My GTM chassis panels were first tacked in place with hot melt glue then held rigidly by a bead of body filler along the seam. The panels were then permanently bonded together, first with a 75mm wide strip of CSM and resin on each seam, then later by two full layers of 600g/m² CSM over the whole interior surface of the chassis *(Pic 2)*.

Nuts and bolts

Nuts and bolts work well with GRP panels but you must plan for their use when you manufacture the panel. Look at any

A sunroof aperture filled with bonded-in glassfibre sheet. Notice the stiffening ribs for the roof panel and windscreen edge and the Kevlar reinforcing for the sun visors (arrowed).

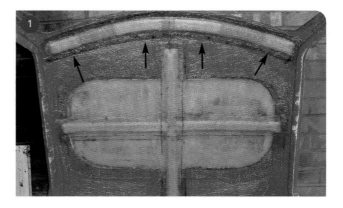

GTM chassis panels held in place with filler, then bonded together with strips of CSM.

older GRP car and you are likely to find crazing or cracking of the gelcoat in certain areas *(Pic 3)*.

These cracks are caused by the GRP flexing in use due to the stresses caused by body movement, hinges, handles and locks. They can be avoided by correct design of the panel in the first place and correct mounting of any fixtures and fittings before use. The key to mounting glassfibre is to spread any loads over the largest possible area. Before you begin any lamination make sure that you know where any mounting points and fittings will be on the finished panel. Plan to add at least two extra layers of 600g/m² CSM in these areas during the moulding process. A layer of Kevlar cloth or tape can help too, as it will prevent the fixing bolts from fretting and enlarging the holes in use. The reinforcing layers should extend at least 50mm around the mounting holes to spread the loads sufficiently *(Pic 4)*.

When you bolt on any fittings, spread the load by using large washers under the bolt heads or nuts. If possible use rubber gaskets under hinges and door locks. The gelcoat is much softer than steel and will wear away if there is any fretting or movement between the parts.

It is quite common to find production car body panels held in place by captive nuts or studs. They are usually spot welded to the panel or fixing bracket. Simply gluing a nut or bolt to a GRP panel is unlikely to produce a strong fixing and will certainly concentrate stress in a very small area, leading to cracking and crazing. Fortunately there is an alternative. A company called 'bigHead Bonding Fasteners' produces a full range of nuts, bolts, studs, threaded sleeves and many other types of fasteners pre-welded to large mounting plates of drilled steel or heavy mesh. These can be incorporated into the laminate during fabrication or glued to the finished laminate at a later date *(Pic 5)*.

The mounting plates spread the load over a large area and ensure a strong bond to the panel. They are available in mild or stainless steel and bigHead can also supply a suitable bonding adhesive if required. If you check their catalogue or website there will be something there to meet your needs.

Adhesives

Modern adhesives are a viable alternative to threaded fasteners and, in some cases, can even replace spot welding for steel panels. They are also capable of bonding dissimilar materials and are ideal for attaching a GRP scoop or bulge to a steel bonnet or roof. Body filler will eventually crack under these circumstances as the different materials flex and expand at different rates. There are two basic types of adhesives commonly available. The simplest to use are the single component polyurethane adhesives such as Sikaflex or Tigerseal which are applied like a mastic or sealant but which set to form a strong flexible bond. They can be painted but the flexibility may cause the paint to crack at a later date. The second type of structural adhesives is the toughened epoxies. They are supplied as two individual components which, when mixed in the correct proportion, set to form a very strong rigid bond between the panels. I have personal experience of these. I used Araldite 2015 to bond together the GRP body and chassis of my GTM Coupé, as well as bonding in suspension mountings, bonnet hinges, catch plates and various brackets. It is designed for GRP and dissimilar materials, has a long working time and is very forgiving in

Gelcoat crazing caused by flexing of the window aperture due to insufficient support in the panel.

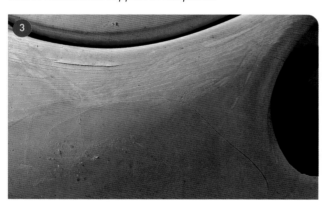

This is a mounting point for a boot handle and locking mechanism. The area is reinforced by extra layers of CSM and Kevlar.

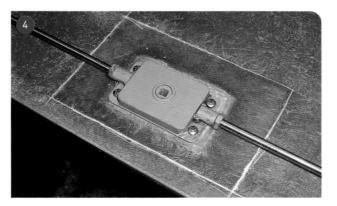

A selection of bigHead fasteners designed to be bonded to a panel or incorporated into the laminate. These are stainless steel.

use. If you are bonding small parts or may want to remove bonded components at a later date, it is worth considering bathroom type silicone sealant. It forms a weaker more flexible bond than polyurethane or structural adhesives and can be removed by suitable solvents if required.

Screws and rivets

Self-tapping screws are designed to work in sheet metal panels. Glassfibre is a soft material and self-tapping screws will not hold for long. Vibration and constant tension will cause the screws to enlarge the holes in the glassfibre and they will quickly work loose. Eventually the thread formed by the screw will strip out completely. If you must use self-tapping screws in a particular application then use spire clips in the GRP panel and you should have no problems (Pic 6).

Pop rivets are also designed to be used in sheet metal. When used in glassfibre they simply enlarge the hole or split the panel as they expand and they lose the tension needed to produce a secure fixing. If there is access to the rear of the panel, and the rivet has sufficient free length, a washer can be used behind the GRP. This takes the mounting stress away from the glassfibre, leaving it sandwiched between the washer and the bracket or fixing (Pic 7).

Rivnuts have become very popular as a means of providing a threaded fixing in a panel, tube or bracket (Pic 8). Unfortunately, like pop rivets, they are designed for use in sheet metal rather than GRP. They may damage the panel as they expand during fitting or work loose in use as the GRP frets away. If you wish to use rivnuts in glassfibre then glue them in with an epoxy adhesive and carefully expand them just enough to locate them till the glue sets.

A better alternative, if you need to use threaded fasteners in GRP panels, is to use screw in threaded inserts (Pic 9). They require a larger hole than a rivnut but provide a much more secure fixing, especially if an epoxy adhesive is used as well. An Allen key is used to screw the insert into the panel leaving a strong threaded boss visible on the surface. These inserts are unlikely to work loose or pull through.

The key to securely and permanently attaching or joining GRP panels is to select the most suitable fixing method first then to design or modify the panels around the fixing method chosen. I hope that the information in this chapter will help you to accomplish this successfully.

These spire clips attach to GRP panels and provide a permanent secure fixing for self tapping screws.

Two types of rivnuts are shown here but neither is particularly suitable for use in glassfibre.

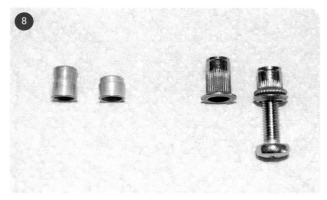

The rivet compresses the GRP panel between the bracket and the washer, giving a much more durable fixing.

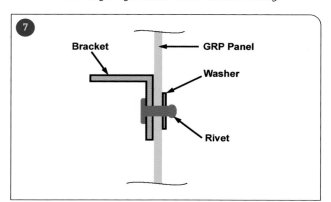

These threaded inserts work well in GRP and can also be used in wood and other soft materials.

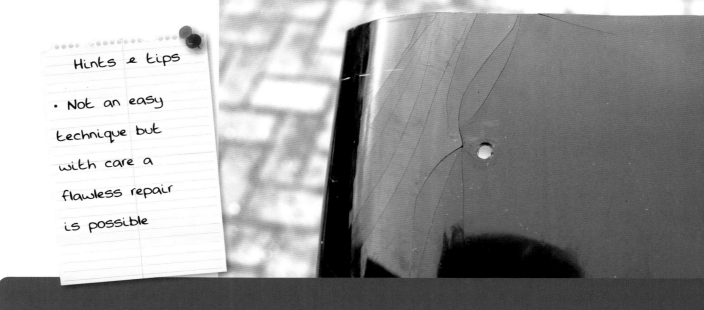

12 Gelcoat Repairs

Cracks, grazing, scratches and blisters

One of the major advantages of GRP is that it can be self-coloured so that no further finishing is necessary. The gelcoat surface is generally harder and more durable than a painted finish too. It also offers financial benefits for the customer. Although the option of a coloured gelcoat finish will add a small premium to the price of the article, due to the extra preparation required for the moulds, the extra care needed with the gelcoat application and the small extra cost of the pigment itself this will be nowhere near the cost of having the item professionally painted. If we are talking about a complete car bodyshell, for example, a professional paint job can easily add £1500 or more to the final build cost.

Unfortunately there are disadvantages too. A self-coloured gelcoat finish is much trickier to repair than a paint finish. In addition, gelcoat resins can be affected by UV light and exposure to the air. Unless they are looked after, a white 'chalky' film will form on the gelcoat surface *(Pic 1)*. This oxidation can be removed in its early stages, but if left too long can cause permanent damage.

The pigments used to colour the gelcoat can also be affected by light in the same way as paint pigments. Older red colours were particularly susceptible to fading, allowing the dark coloured lay-up resin to show through the gelcoat. This gives the unfortunate appearance of a badly brush painted finish. Accurately matching and touching up faded gelcoat colours is practically impossible, as the range of gelcoat pigments is much smaller than the range of tints available to paint suppliers. There are steps that can be taken to preserve or restore gelcoat, though, and these will be dealt with in the next section of this chapter.

Gelcoat care and restoration

Apart from actual physical damage, the main cause for concern with gelcoat finishes is the detrimental effect of UV light. As already described, the gelcoat colour can fade and

A Mini Marcos showing typical gelcoat deterioration caused by UV exposure.

the gelcoat itself can oxidise to form a white bloom or coating on its surface. Keeping the car in a garage when not in use will delay the onset of these problems, as will a good quality car cover but, in the end, if you drive your car regularly it is bound to be exposed to the elements. Many of the modern car waxes provide a temporary UV barrier and will help if used regularly, but the best results will be obtained by using products specifically designed for GRP surfaces. These are not commonly available through motor factors but can be easily obtained from Marine suppliers or Chandlers. Various products are available but Farecla are a well known brand and their products are commonly used in automotive body shops too. They produce Farecla Marine Gel Coat Restorer, a mildly abrasive compound for removing the white bloom or chalking. They have Farecla Marine Gel Coat Restorer & Wax which polishes off the chalking and leaves a wax coating behind, and finally they produce Farecla Marine Ultimate UV Wax which is designed specifically to protect gelcoat surfaces against oxidation and UV attack.

If your gelcoat surface is in good condition the Ultimate UV Wax, used regularly, should help to keep it that way. If there is some slight chalkiness the Gel Coat Restorer should be used to polish away the oxidation leaving a clean gelcoat surface which should then be protected by the wax. If the oxidation will not easily polish away, a last resort is to try rubbing down the surface with 800 then 1200 grit wet and dry paper and polishing it back to a shine with rubbing compound and T-Cut or one of the Farecla polishes. Try a small area first to see if this treatment will produce the desired result. If the gelcoat colour itself has faded then no amount of polishing or waxing will cure the problem and ultimately painting the car may be your only option.

Repairing gelcoat damage

Before you start any sort of remedial work on the gelcoat you need to be sure that you can obtain a suitable supply of a pigment which will enable you to satisfactorily match your gelcoat repair to the existing colour. It may be that the original manufacturer can supply you with a small quantity

These spider cracks have been repaired and filled with gelcoat resin. The car will ultimately be painted, so there is no need to colour match the repair.

of pigment or tinted gelcoat resin. If not, they may be able to tell you the name or colour code for the pigment so that you can purchase your own. If you cannot match the current colour then any repair, no matter how well done, will be visible unless painted. If you cannot find a paint colour to exactly match the existing gelcoat colour then you will not be able to blend the repair successfully into the surrounding finish and you may end up painting the whole panel or car. Even if you are successful in obtaining what should be the correct colour for your component, you need to check it against a cleaned area of the panel to be sure that it still matches. If your panel is more than a couple of years old there is a possibility that its colour may have changed significantly and the 'correct' pigment will no longer match.

If your item is already painted then any colour matching problems are transferred to the paint rather than the gelcoat but this is likely to be easier as there is a much wider range of paint colours available than gelcoat pigments. Before attempting any repairs, all the old paint must be removed from the damaged area. Use abrasive paper rather than paint stripper as most paint strippers will attack the gelcoat. There are some paint strippers which claim to be suitable for glassfibre but even these have to be used with great care. I prefer not to use these chemicals just to be on the safe side. With the paint removed, the gelcoat repairs can be carried out as described below and the area can then be repainted to produce an invisible repair just as for a steel panel *(Pic 2)*.

A tip for painting any new GRP surface or fresh body filler is to leave it to fully cure for a couple of days before any paint is applied. If 'green' glassfibre or filler is painted, the thinners in the paint will sink into the new surface leaving visible marks in the final paint finish.

Repairing gelcoat scratches

A simple scratch in the gelcoat is fairly easy to repair. If there is no damage to the underlying glassfibre the scratches can simply be filled with gelcoat resin or paste tinted to match the original colour *(Pics 3 and 4)*.

If the scratches are old they may need cleaning with acetone or thinners to remove and dirt and grease. Masking off the area

These scratches are purely cosmetic and can be filled with tinted gelcoat. There are no structural repairs needed.

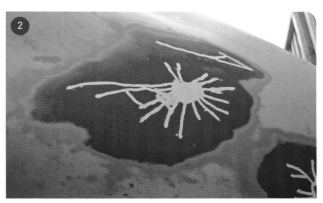

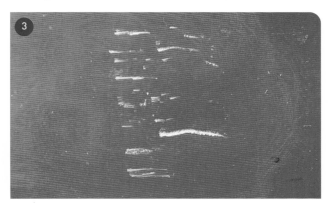

around the scratch will help to control the spread of the resin and will reduce the work involved in the finishing process *(Pic 5)*.

A small amount of gelcoat, about one teaspoon full, would be needed for a repair of this size. The pigment is added and mixed in well. Remember a maximum of 10% pigment should be used or it can affect the setting of the resin. Finally, a couple of drops of catalyst should be stirred in and the resin is then ready for use. Using a small paintbrush or cocktail stick, the resin should be painted into the scratches making sure that all of the damage is well covered *(Pic 6)*.

The resin should be left slightly proud of the surface so that it can be sanded smooth when set *(Pic 7)*.

If gelcoat resin is left exposed to the air it will stay sticky on the surface. A small piece of polyester film or polythene taped over the repair will exclude the air and allow the gelcoat to set solid *(Pic 8)*.

These scratches in my sample panel were made using a convenient brick wall.

Masking the surrounding area will avoid mess and save time later.

The matching resin is carefully painted in to fill the scratches.

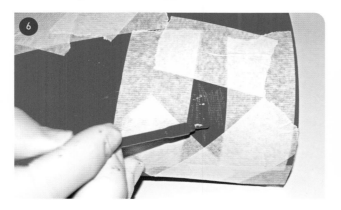

The gelcoat resin should be left proud of the original surface to allow for finishing.

A small piece of polyester film is taped over the resin to exclude air so that it will set correctly.

The polyester film has smoothed out the surface of the resin beautifully.

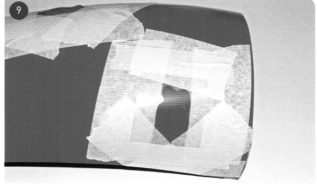

The polyester film will also smooth out the gelcoat surface, meaning that less rubbing down will be needed when it has set *(Pic 9)*. Polythene tends to wrinkle in contact with resin so it will not have the same smoothing effect on the gelcoat surface.

Allow the gelcoat plenty of time to fully harden, then carefully remove the release film. It should peel away easily leaving a smooth hard surface *(Pic 10)*.

With the film removed, the smooth surface can be seen.

A small file is easier to control than sandpaper. At this stage the masking tape is left on to protect the finish.

Using the paper on a block will help you to sand only the area required.

The masking tape is left in place at this stage to protect the surrounding area. A small file is useful for the initial shaping. It removes the material quickly but is easy to control and less likely to damage the rest of the gelcoat *(Pic 11)*.

When you start to file into the masking tape remove it and, taking extra care, file the repair almost flush with the surface. Using 400 grit wet & dry paper on a small block, flat the repair down until the surface is smooth *(Pic 12)*.

This is the finished repair. It is almost invisible even on close inspection.

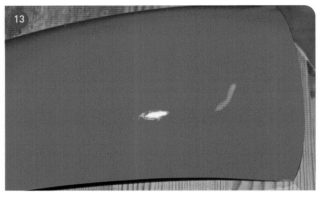

These stress cracks were caused by an impact at the opposite end of the mudguard, causing flex at the fixing bracket.

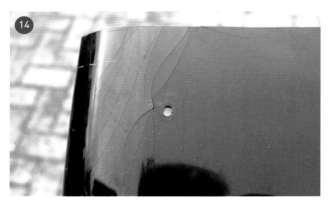

The rear of the panel shows the real damage. The gelcoat has separated from the laminate where the white lines are visible.

Use progressively finer grades of abrasive to smooth the gelcoat. 600 and 800 grit papers will be fine. Finish with 1200 grit then polish the surface to a gloss with a mildly abrasive polish such as T-Cut or one of the Farecla range. If you have taken enough care the repair should be practically invisible (Pic 13).

Obviously this is a time consuming process even on a small repair like this. Repairing larger scratches will take a lot of time and will need great care but this technique is the only way to achieve a successful cosmetic repair on a gelcoat finish.

Repairing stress cracks and star (or spider) crazing

Stress cracks are caused by the laminate flexing near mountings, hinges, locks or handles. The glassfibre flexes under the strain but the gelcoat is more brittle and cracks. The stress cracks in this MNR Vortx mudguard have probably been caused by the nearby mounting bracket. On first glance they seem quite minor (Pic 14).

The rear of the panel shows the true extent of the damage. The white lines are the cracks where the gelcoat has separated from the laminate (Pic 15).

Star crazing, which often appears on mudguards and wings, is caused by the impact of small stones (or tools) on the underside of the glassfibre. The impact damages the laminate and the resulting distortion causes the gelcoat to crack (Pic 16).

Although the damage looks quite minor, the fact that an impact below the GRP has caused damage to appear on the upper surface means that the glassfibre structure has actually been damaged all the way through.

The repair process is the same for both stress cracks and star crazing. The first step is to prevent any further flexing or damage by reinforcing the GRP laminate from below.

A fine example of star crazing (along with oxidation, micro-blistering and possible chemical attack all in the same small area).

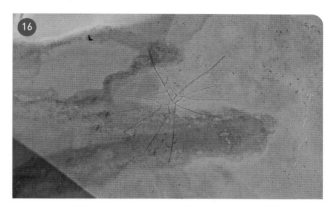

The area behind the star crazing is keyed so that the repair will bond to the original GRP.

An ideal set-up for abrading GRP to provide a key for further layers of glassfibre.

The keyed area is painted with catalysed resin.

Resin is stippled into the first layer of CSM.

The area behind this star crazing shows the damaged laminate. The area is first roughened to provide a key for the new resin and CSM. The roughened area shows how much overlap there will be in the repair *(Pic 17)*.

A twist knot brush mounted in an angle grinder is the perfect tool for keying the GRP prior to the repair but a sanding disc in a drill or abrasive paper used by hand will work eventually. You may need to remove hinges or fittings from the panel in order to get sufficient access for a successful repair *(Pic 18)*.

At least two layers of 600g/m^2 CSM need to be laminated on to the rear of the panel to restore the strength lost by the impact damage. A thin coat of resin is first painted onto the rear of the panel as usual *(Pic 19)*.

The first layer of CSM is stippled in place over the damage. Once it is wetted out and becomes transparent it can be re-positioned centrally over the damage if necessary *(Pic 20)*.

The layers of CSM need to extend beyond the area of the visible damage by at least 25mm all round to adequately

The second layer overlaps the first by about 25mm all round.

The roller is used to fully wet out and consolidate the repair.

The finished lamination showing how far it overlaps the original damage.

The area behind the stress cracks on the MNR mudguard showing the reinforcement which will prevent any further flex.

Once the glassfibre has set, the gelcoat repairs can begin.

Using a cutting wheel in a rotary tool to cut away the damaged gelcoat.

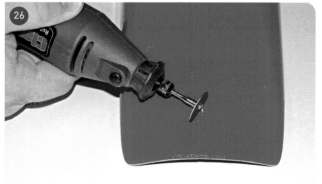

reinforce the damage. *(Pic 21)* Even on a small area like this it is worth using the roller to fully consolidate the layers of CSM. The finished repair will be neater and stronger *(Pic 22)*.

Check the finished lamination for air bubbles and make sure the patches are correctly positioned over the damage then allow the resin to cure fully before moving onto the next step *(Pic 23)*.

The repair on the MNR mudguard is carried out in exactly the same way and the resulting repair reinforces the panel to prevent any further flex *(Pic 24)*.

When you are satisfied that the resin has cured and the repaired area is rigid enough you can move on to tackle the damaged gelcoat *(Pic 25)*.

All the cracked gelcoat and damaged CSM must be removed before new gelcoat can be painted in. A small

Opening out the cracks using a small grind stone in the same rotary tool.

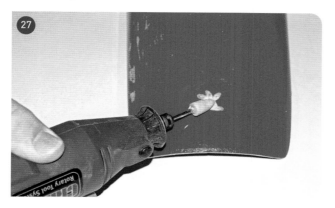

A toy paintbrush is perfect for a repair of this size. The fine glass strands are cut from a piece of woven roving.

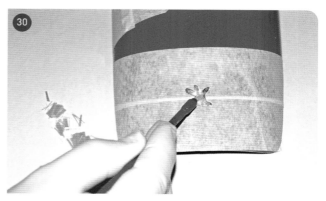

The cracks opened out and damaged glassfibre cut away. At this point the repair can begin.

The fine strands of glassfibre are too small to pick up by hand. Use the brush to pick them up and position them.

Masking off the area around the repair will save time later on.

Ideally the repair should end up below the level of the gelcoat, but in this case one or two strands got away.

Dremel type tool with a cutting disc is perfect for this (Pic 26) but a hacksaw blade, file tang or Stanley knife blade can be used too.

The cracks need to be opened out so that new glassfibre can be laminated into them to restore the strength and thickness. If you just fill the cracks with gelcoat it will be too thick and will quickly crack away in use. The Dremel tool fitted with a shaped grind stone works well here (Pic 27).

The masking tape will avoid sticky fingerprints and speed up finishing later.

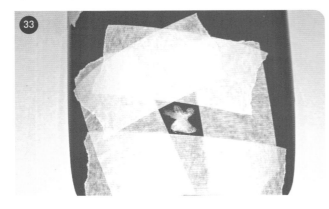

The resin should cover the whole of the damage and also extend over the edges slightly.

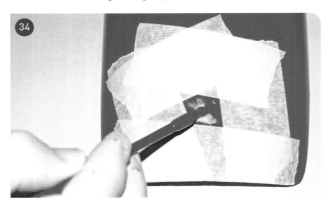

The gelcoat resin will set with a hard surface as the release film excludes air from the repair.

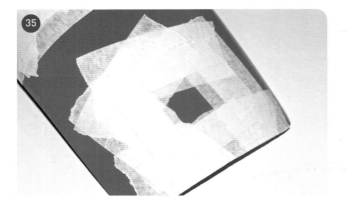

Open out the cracks and grind away any split or damaged CSM. It doesn't matter if you have to grind all the way through to the new glassfibre on the rear of the panel. Delaminated CSM fibres will prevent a proper repair and must all be removed before lamination begins (Pic 28).

If you mask off the area around the repair before you paint on the lay-up resin, you will have less cleaning up and sanding to do to achieve the final finish (Pic 29).

Use a small paintbrush to laminate in thin strips of CSM or, in this case, fine strands of glassfibre cut from a piece of woven roving. Saturate them fully with resin as you would for any lamination (Pic 30).

Use the brush to pick up the small strands and place them into the repair. If you try to use your fingers, or gloves, you will end up with most of the material stuck to your hands and very little on the actual workpiece (Pic 31).

Ideally, when you are finished, the repair should end up slightly below the level of the surrounding surface so that you can paint in a thin layer of colour matched gelcoat to level the surface ready for final finishing. In this example one or two strands will need to be levelled before the gelcoat is applied (Pic 32).

When the lay-up resin has set, the odd strands of glass are cleaned up with the small grind stone and the repair area is re-masked ready for the gelcoat to be painted in (Pic 33).

This is the finished repair. The time and effort needed is reflected in the final result.

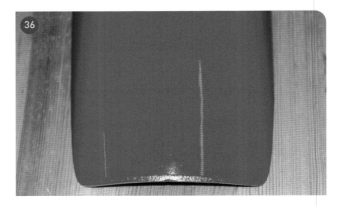

This bubble was deliberately produced in order to demonstrate this repair technique.

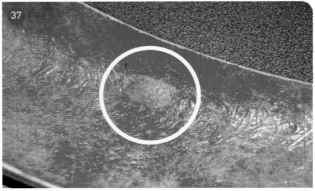

The tinted and catalysed gelcoat resin is carefully painted in to the prepared area, leaving it just proud of the original surface so that it can be smoothed down and polished to match the surrounding gelcoat *(Pic 34)*.

Polyester film is carefully taped over the liquid resin. This excludes the air, allowing the resin to set with a non-sticky surface and also smooths out the resin making it easier to sand and polish when it has set *(Pic 35)*.

On the outer surface of the mudguard there is a corresponding raised area which is flexible and clearly unsupported.

The blister cracks easily as it is only a thin layer of gelcoat.

This shows the full extent of the blister.

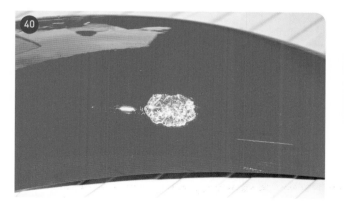

When the resin has fully hardened, the polyester film can be removed and the gelcoat resin can be carefully shaped, smoothed and polished. This process is described in detail in the previous section on stress cracks and spider crazing *(Pic 36)*.

Once again the process is time consuming and great care is needed but the results can be well worth the effort.

Repairing blisters

GRP boat hulls suffer from a problem called osmosis. If the gelcoat is micro-porous, or damaged, water can penetrate through to the laminate below and cause it to separate from the gelcoat. Blisters will appear on the gelcoat surface.

In the automotive field gelcoat blisters are more likely to be caused by poor laminating technique and, unfortunately, are not unknown even in brand new bodyshells or panels. In the chapters describing fabrication I stressed the importance of consolidating the matting thoroughly onto the gelcoat to avoid dry patches, bubbles or voids. If this is not done and bubbles of air remain in the lamination they will show up as blisters on the outer gelcoat surface. In order to demonstrate this particular repair I deliberately (honestly!) allowed an air bubble to remain in the lamination of a small mudguard section *(Pic 37)*.

On the outer surface these air bubbles are visible as

Masking the area around the repair will save time later.

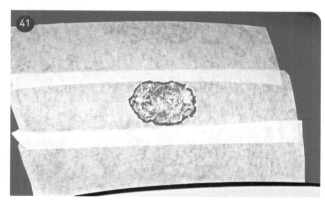

Small pieces of CSM are laminated into the blister to strengthen the repair.

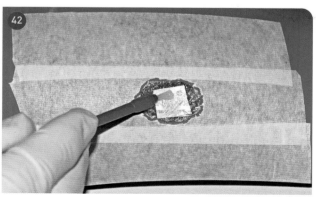

blisters in the gelcoat which will be raised up slightly and are flexible. If you push them in they will spring back up *(Pic 38)*.

You can ignore these defects for a while but no matter how carefully you clean or polish round them they will eventually crack, so you may as well bite the bullet and crack them yourself, then repair them properly with strips of CSM, resin

The finished lamination should be just below the level of the surrounding gelcoat to allow a final layer of tinted gelcoat to be painted in.

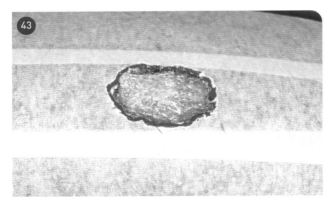

Once again the area is masked to avoid mess and save time.

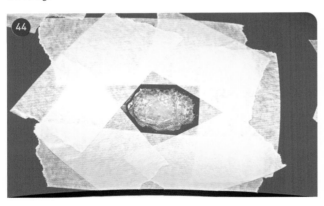

The resin will sag slightly on this vertical surface but it will not run significantly and the polyester film will keep it in place until it sets.

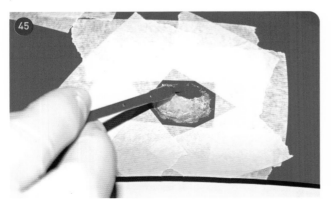

and new gelcoat. Fortunately, since there is no damage to the underlying lamination, you can simply repair the gelcoat layer with no need for additional reinforcement below the panel *(Pic 39)*.

Once the blister is cracked all the unsupported gelcoat needs to be removed to expose the CSM below. Any loose strands of CSM also need to be cut away *(Pic 40)*.

The depression formed needs to be filled with small pieces of CSM and resin until it is almost flush with the surface. You cannot fill a hole this deep with gelcoat alone. It would quickly crack away from the laminate below. Masking off the surrounding area will save time cleaning up later *(Pic 41)*.

Small pieces of CSM about 10mm square are perfect for this repair. They are laminated into the blister using a small paintbrush. As the lay-up resin dissolves the binder in the CSM, the pieces will change shape to fit into the repair *(Pic 42)*.

Ideally the CSM should be laminated into the blister until it is just below the level of the surrounding gelcoat. This will allow for a thin coating of colour matched gelcoat resin to be painted into the repair as described in the preceding sections *(Pic 43)*.

When the lay-up resin has set it is a good idea to re-mask the surrounding area, as described earlier, before the tinted and catalysed gelcoat resin is added *(Pic 44)*.

The polyester film in place. The smooth surface will be easier and quicker to sand down.

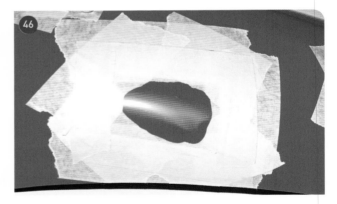

The small white mark is a bubble which I accidentally left in the repair. This would need further work.

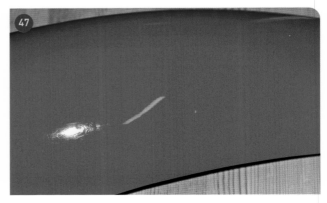

As before, the tinted gelcoat is painted on to fill the repair and is left standing proud of the original surface so that it can be sanded flush when set *(Pic 45)*.

The polyester release film is flexible but has no stretch. This particular panel has a double curvature in this area so it is trickier to get the film perfectly smooth. This is no great problem, since it will be sanded down later anyway *(Pic 46)*.

When the resin has cured, the film can be removed and the repair can be carefully rubbed down and polished. This is done in exactly the same way as in the earlier section on stress cracks and spider crazing. When I sanded this particular repair to shape a hole appeared. This was a bubble which, in spite of my care, I had left in the gelcoat resin as I was painting it into the repair *(Pic 47)*.

Apart from this blemish, the finish is excellent and this small hole, produced by the bubble, could easily be repaired with more gelcoat, but it is annoying to have to carry out remedial work on what is repair anyway. More care on my part would have avoided the need for this.

Hiding the damage

It may be that, for whatever reason, a successful gelcoat repair is not possible. A possible alternative may be to hide the damage under a trim or cover. This GTM Libra had sustained fairly typical damage around the exhaust pipe exit port due to movement of the engine on its mountings *(Pic 48)*.

Unfortunately, the owner had been unable to obtain a reasonable quantity of a matching pigment and had also been unsuccessful in finding a good paint match. I suggested that, as an alternative, we may be able to hide the damage with a suitable trim and he agreed to try this option. The damage was repaired temporarily with filler and the surrounding area was cleaned and polished to give a smooth finish. A suitable area was masked off and treated with PVA release agent, then laminated with gelcoat and three layers of CSM to form a female mould *(Pic 49)*.

When this had cured it was removed from the vehicle, trimmed and cleaned. There were one or two minor defects on this mould surface and these were sanded smooth with 1200 grit wet and dry paper and polished up with T-Cut *(Pic 50)*.

The mould was then prepared in the usual way and a thin lamination containing one layer of clear gelcoat, one layer of carbon fibre fabric and one layer of black tinted surface tissue was laid up into the mould. When this had cured it was removed from the mould, trimmed and washed. The finished trim fitted the car well and covered the damage quite neatly *(Pic 51)*.

The exhaust has damaged both the gelcoat and the CSM and the attempt at paint matching has not been successful.

This is the trimmed and polished mould, ready for the release agent. A handle was glued on to make it easier to hold.

The panel surface was prepared correctly with suitable release agents so this mould separated easily leaving no marks or residue on the car.

The completed carbon fibre trim fitted to the car.

Ultimately, I ended up making a number of copies for other owners whose cars had suffered similar damage.

Repairing a damaged gelcoat finish is nothing like as easy as repairing a painted finish but, as I hope I have shown in this chapter, it is still possible for a person with a little skill and a lot of patience to restore damaged glassfibre back to its original strength and its original cosmetic appearance.

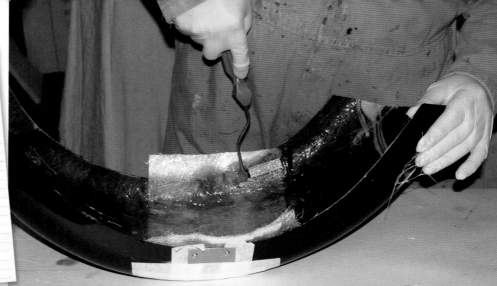

Hints & tips

• Restoring full structural strength to fibreglass panels

13 Structural Repairs

Cracks, breaks and holes

Glassfibre handles impacts in a very different way to steel. Glassfibre is flexible and absorbs impacts either by cracking or by deforming then springing back to shape. Steel is malleable and absorbs impacts by deforming permanently. Glassfibre also localises the structural damage close to the area of the impact whereas steel tends to deform over a much larger area. Glassfibre can be repaired to be as strong as or stronger than the original panel. Steel loses some strength if deformed then straightened, so steel panels are more often replaced than repaired.

The problem with glassfibre is that the actual laminate may be damaged over a larger area than is initially visible. Since it springs back to its original shape after an impact it may appear to be largely undamaged whereas, in fact, the laminate may be split or cracked over a larger area. This MNR

The impact area showing the scuffing and a few fine gelcoat cracks.

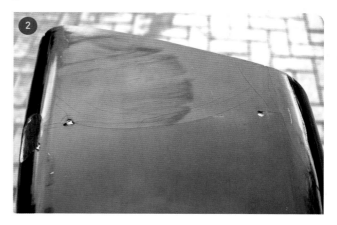

A GRP mudguard from MNR. The impact mark can be seen on the lower front edge.

The rear of the impact area showing how the GRP has flexed and cracked.

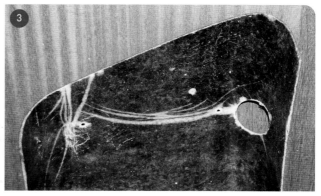

Vortx mudguard has been damaged in a racing incident. At first glance it seems to be relatively unscathed (Pic 1).

An inspection of the damaged area shows some scuffing and gelcoat cracking around the impact area but nothing serious (Pic 2).

Inspection from the rear of the panel, however, reveals

These are stress cracks formed at the rear mounting point of the mudguard.

The massive gelcoat damage visible at the top of this picture is the result of the apparently small impact on the wheel arch of Simon Haydn's GTM Libra.

No attempt has been made to repair this crack. It has simply been skimmed over with filler. The filler has split then cracked away.

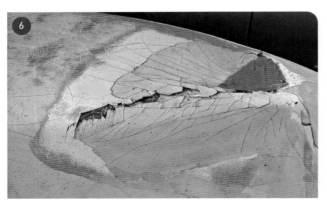

some serious structural damage which would certainly need repairing before this panel could be used again (Pic 3). In fact an examination of the whole mudguard shows that damage has also occurred at the other end too (Pic 4). The first rule then, is to thoroughly inspect a damaged GRP panel on both its inner and outer surfaces to establish the true extent of the damage before considering a repair.

The flexing of the panel on impact can also cause gelcoat damage which may not appear for some time. The gelcoat is brittle and will crack if the panel flexes. These cracks may be quite extensive but may not all appear immediately, so the second rule is, if possible, delay the cosmetic part of the repair until you are sure that all the gelcoat damage has finally appeared (Pic 5).

What can be done?

Repairing a GRP panel is much easier if you have all the pieces. If the panel is cracked or split but is still basically in one piece then the repair will be relatively simple. If the panel is in pieces but all the pieces are available it will still be possible to affect a repair although it is a little trickier. If large pieces are missing from a broken panel, particularly around the perimeter, it may be very difficult to repair the panel to a satisfactory standard and buying or moulding a new panel may be a better option.

How not to do it

There is absolutely no point in trying to skim or fill over damaged glassfibre. The damaged section will have no strength or rigidity and will flex under the slightest load. The filler will split or crack away very quickly (Pic 6).

A proper repair will remove any damaged GRP, restore the strength by laminating in new glassfibre, then repair the gelcoat to restore the surface to its original appearance. If done correctly the repair will be permanent and undetectable. The following examples show how this can be done.

Repairing a cracked panel

If a GRP panel has cracked but all the pieces have remained in place, then the repair is fairly straightforward. You cannot

A panel which is broken but still basically in one piece. The repair is fairly straightforward.

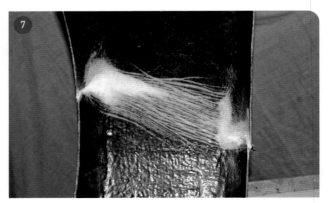

re-laminate damaged GRP but you can use it to keep the panel in shape while it is being repaired. The fracture in this mudguard is typical of this type of damage and will be used to demonstrate this repair (Pic 7).

Any loose strands of broken glassfibre need to be cut away from the damaged area. They can jam against each other preventing the panel from returning to its correct shape and can also interfere with the new laminate (Pic 8).

These loose strands and broken shards need to be cut away back to sound glassfibre. They cannot be re-laminated.

The cutting disc on the angle grinder will quickly remove the damaged glassfibre.

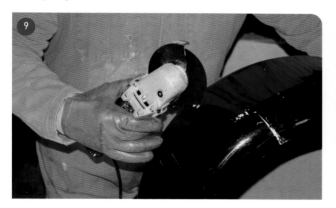

This is the rear of the panel fully keyed for the repair. The loose GRP strands have been removed.

An angle grinder fitted with a cutting wheel is ideal for this. Always use gloves and eye protection when using power tools (Pic 9).

The rear of the panel needs to be roughened with an abrasive disc or rotary wire brush to provide a good key for the repair. A large area each side of the damage needs to be keyed, as the panel will be reinforced over as wide an area as possible (Pic 10).

The GRP cleat will be used to support the panel during the repair. Self tapping screws will hold the cleats in place temporarily.

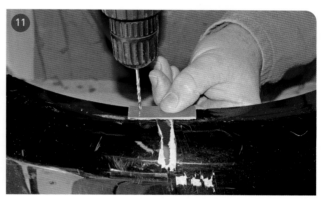

This polyester release film will seal the gap and provide a backing for the new GRP.

The polyester release film is taped into position.

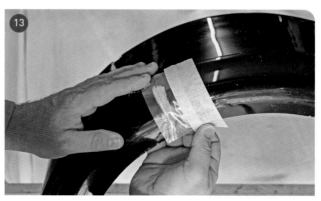

Once the damaged glassfibre has been removed, the panel is no longer rigid. It needs to be held in shape during the repair or it will be permanently distorted. A couple of small glassfibre cleats screwed or glued to the panel will hold it in position while the new GRP is laminated into the repair but

This side of the mudguard is ready for the new glassfibre. The polyester film, tape and cleats are in position and the panel will be held securely until the new GRP cures.

The polyester film should follow the panel contours as closely as possible. This will minimise the smoothing and finishing required.

Tinted gelcoat has been painted into the areas where the loose GRP was cut away. This may give us a start on the gelcoat repairs when the CSM has cured.

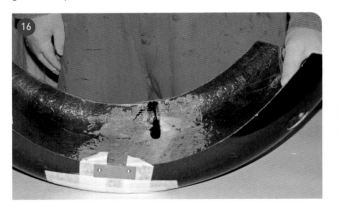

make sure the panel is correctly aligned when you mark and fix the cleats *(Pic 11)*.

The holes left by removal of the damaged CSM need to be sealed so that new glassfibre can be laminated into them without the resin running through. This can be done with tape, polythene or polyester release film. Polyester film is designed for the job and will produce the best results. A small piece of the film is first cut to size *(Pic 12)*.

The film is taped into position, keeping it as smooth as possible then more tape is used to back up the film and keep it fairly rigid *(Pic 13)*.

The cleats are then screwed into place to keep the panel held firmly in shape *(Pic 14)*.

The polyester film should follow the contours of the panel as closely as possible to minimise the amount of smoothing and finishing needed after the repair *(Pic 15)*.

Gelcoat resin is painted into the areas where the damaged original laminate was cut away. This reinforces the release film and also seals the gaps so that the lay-up resin does not leak through *(Pic 16)*.

If necessary, the keyed area can be degreased with acetone or thinners, then lay-up resin and CSM can be laminated over the damaged area. The final repair needs to be at least as thick as the original panel, so three layers of 600g/m^2 matting

The first layer of CSM ready to be saturated with lay-up resin.

Stippling the resin into the CSM thoroughly using a brush.

will be used here. The first piece of matting should overlap the repair area by at least 25mm all round *(Pic 17)*.

The resin should be thoroughly stippled into the CSM in the usual way for each layer of matting *(Pic 18)*.

Each successive layer should also overlap the previous one by around 25mm each side *(Pic 19 and 20)*.

To fully wet out three layers of CSM and resin and to remove air bubbles, a roller is recommended. It will consolidate the layers of matting giving the repair the maximum possible strength *(Pic 21)*.

Before finally cleaning out the tools and container, check the final repair for dry patches or air bubbles, particularly near the edges *(Pic 22)*.

Allow the repair to cure then remove the tape, release film and cleats from the front of the panel and trim away any excess glassfibre *(Pic 23)*.

This is the second layer of CSM showing the degree of overlap.

This is the completed repair ready to be set aside to cure.

The third layer overlaps the previous two by a similar amount.

The laminate has cured, the tape, screws and cleats have been removed and the excess glassfibre has been trimmed.

A roller is recommended to wet out and consolidate three layers of CSM and resin.

All the damaged glassfibre and cracked gelcoat will need to be cut away and repaired. This is the most time consuming part of the repair.

Moving to the front of the panel, any remaining damaged glassfibre or gelcoat now needs to be cut away. This can be done with a cutting wheel, hacksaw blade, file or any suitable tool *(Pic 24)*.

The rest of the repair is described in detail in Chapter 12. The gelcoat cracks are opened out and thin strips of glassfibre are laminated into them. Tinted gelcoat resin or repair paste is painted in to fill the cracks and this is smoothed and finished with progressively finer abrasive papers and polishes.

Repairing a broken panel

If the panel has suffered an impact large enough to break it into a number of pieces but all the pieces are present, then the repair is trickier but still possible. You just need to be very good at jigsaws. Basically, using tape, glue, screws, cleats and any other temporary fixing system that works, you have to reassemble all the broken pieces to reform the shape of the original panel as perfectly as possible. You may need to trim away broken edges to get them to fit back together correctly but remember the most important consideration at this stage is getting the shape of the panel correct. The strength of the repair will come from the new glassfibre that you will laminate onto the rear of the panel once the shape

is achieved. Once you have all the pieces in place and you are happy with the contours of the panel, the actual repair is carried out exactly as described in the previous section of this chapter. The rear of the panel is prepared and layers of CSM are laminated on until the required strength is achieved. The gelcoat on the outer surface is repaired as described, in detail, in Chapter 12.

If there are any small pieces missing from the panel it may be possible to cover the resulting hole with polyester film backed up by tape, cardboard or thin GRP sheet providing the missing section is a relatively simple shape. It may also be possible to cover a hole with a small partial mould made from another part of the panel or car to re-mould the missing area. These techniques are described in more detail in the next section of this chapter covering the repair of a hole.

If the damage to the panel is extensive it may be easier to make a new one. A temporary repair is carried out using the broken parts, glue, foam, filler and primer then the repaired panel is used as a plug to make a full or partial mould as described in Chapter 6. This mould can then be used to manufacture a completely new panel or panel section. If replacement body panels are no longer available for your vehicle this may be your only option *(Pic 25)*.

This Mini Marcos bonnet was run over. A full repair will be very involved and moulding a new panel may be a better option.

Diagram to show the structure of a repair on a hole in fibreglass

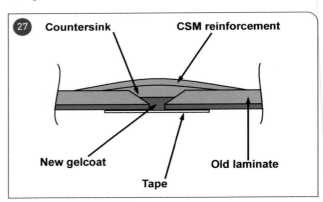

This screw hole has been countersunk. It will be filled with gelcoat and a GRP patch will reinforce the inside.

The area to the right of the hole has been polished with T-Cut.

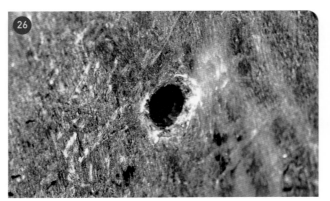

Repairing a hole in a panel

A small hole left behind from a screw or bolt is simple to repair. From the rear of the panel the hole is countersunk slightly using a large drill and the glassfibre surface is abraded to provide a key for the repair (Pic 26).

On the front of the panel the hole is sealed with tape or polyester release film following the shape of the panel as closely as possible. Working at the rear of the panel again, the hole is filled with a small amount of catalysed and tinted gelcoat resin then, when this has set, one or two layers of CSM are laminated over the repair to support the gelcoat (Pic 27).

This same procedure can be used to repair larger holes too but as the size of the hole increases it becomes more difficult to follow the contours of the panel with tape or

The prepared section is masked off.

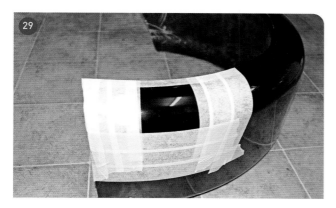

The prepared section is treated with PVA.

Only one layer of CSM has been used so that the partial mould will be flexible enough to bend slightly if necessary.

The partial mould will be treated with PVA then clamped or taped in this position.

This is the inner surface keyed ready for the application of the glassfibre. The edges of the hole have been feathered to a fine edge.

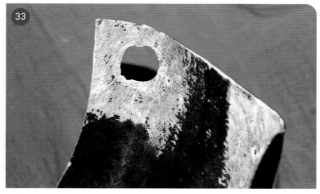

The partial mould has been treated with PVA and carefully positioned over the hole.

polyester film and the repair will probably need some filling and finishing. It may, however, be possible to get a better result by making a partial mould for the repair from another part of the panel.

The MNR Vortx mudguard will once again be ideal to demonstrate this. The contours of the mudguard are fairly constant and there is an area just to the right of the hole which may be suitable to make a partial mould *(Pic 28)*.

The area chosen is prepared by polishing or smoothing with very fine abrasive then masked off to avoid spilling resin on the rest of the panel *(Pic 29)*. PVA release agent is then

The partial mould has been securely taped in position to provide a secure backing for the repair.

Two circles of CSM are laminated into the hole to bring the repair flush with the rest of the panel.

Viewed from the reverse of the panel the fit of the mould looks good. The feathering on the edges of the hole can also be seen. The next step is to paint in a layer of matching gelcoat.

The repair is reinforced with patches of CSM laminated onto the rear of the panel.

Black tinted gelcoat has been painted onto the partial mould.

The resin is stippled into the CSM in the usual way using a small brush.

applied to the area and allowed to dry (Pic 30).

Gelcoat resin and CSM are then laminated onto the area and allowed to cure (Pic 31).

The partial mould can then be lifted off the mudguard, trimmed and cleaned up. The mudguard itself is also cleaned up ready for the repair (Pic 32).

The rear of the panel needs to be cleaned up and abraded to form a key for the repair. The edges of the hole also need to be filed or sanded to a taper to avoid a step or ledge in the repair (Pic 33).

The partial mould is then treated with PVA release agent and clamped or taped over the hole as tightly as possible (Pics 34 and 35).

The mould needs to fit as tightly as possible to the panel so that the contours of the repair will match the original panel and so that resin cannot leak between the mould and the panel (Pic 36).

Working from the reverse of the panel, tinted gelcoat is painted into the hole and allowed to cure (Pic 37).

The hole is then filled with two layers of resin and CSM cut to the same size and shape as the hole (Pic 38).

The rear of the panel is then built up using larger pieces of CSM which are used to reinforce the area, overlapping the hole by around 25mm all round (Pic 39).

The second layer should overlap the first by about 25mm. The resin should be applied and stippled into the CSM using a brush in the usual way (Pic 40).

Even though the repair area is quite small there are four layers of CSM and resin here, so the roller will help to squeeze the resin throughout the CSM giving more strength to the repair (Pic 41).

The repair should be checked for air bubbles or dry spots then allowed to fully cure before the next step. (Pic 42).

Once the structural repair has cured, the panel should be as strong as or stronger than it was before the damage. The extent of the overlap can be seen on the cured glassfibre (Pic 43).

Moving to the front of the panel, it can be seen that the effort involved in making the partial mould was well worth it. The outer surface of the gelcoat is almost perfectly flush with the original panel and very little finishing will be required to produce a perfect repair (Pic 44).

Fine wet and dry paper, rubbing compound and T-Cut will blend the repair into the original panel with very little effort. The fine gelcoat cracks can be treated as described in the previous chapter. The initial structural part of the repair has already been done so, once opened out, the cracks can be

Even though the repair is quite small a roller will ensure that all four layers of CSM are fully wetted out.

The finished repair ready to be set aside to fully cure.

The extent of the overlap can be seen on the cured glassfibre.

The outer surface of the gelcoat is almost perfectly flush with the original panel and very little finishing will be required to produce a perfect repair

filled with gelcoat or gelcoat filler and blended into the original finish.

Repairing incomplete panels

This is really a last resort if there is no other way of obtaining a replacement. If you have a panel which has been broken and is no longer complete, then the success of your repair will depend mostly on your skill as a sculptor. You need to assemble as much of the panel as you can using whatever original pieces remain then fill in the gaps with GRP sheet, CSM and resin, filler and aluminium gauze. If you can produce something that looks correct on the outside then you can restore the strength of the panel by laminating three or four layers of CSM onto the inside to hold it all together. If even this is not a viable option then you need to use the original panel and the materials previously mentioned along with wood, foam, plaster and any other suitable material to produce a plug. The shape of the plug has to be correct but the structure and strength are unimportant, so you can use easily shaped materials to make the work quicker and easier. You can then make a mould from your plug and finally use the mould to produce a brand new replacement for the damaged item. This process is described in detail in Chapter 8.

Repairing glassfibre to restore its strength is relatively straightforward and certainly easier than steel but restoring its cosmetic appearance to a satisfactory standard is much more time consuming. However if you own a GRP bodied vehicle or one with GRP accessories or trim you will, at some time, find yourself having to repair or re-manufacture parts. Hopefully the information in this book will have given you the knowledge and confidence to successfully complete the job.

Appendix 1
Mixing table

This table will save you some time working out the quantities of resin and hardener required for a particular job.

Roughly work out, in square metres, the area you need to cover. Find the nearest figure to this in the first column in the table. Read off how much gelcoat resin and hardener you will need to cover the workpiece. Read off the amount of lay-up resin and hardener needed for a layer of surface tissue. Read off how much resin and hardener will be needed to wet out each layer of CSM.

I have worked out figures for each of the three commonly available thicknesses of CSM in case you prefer to use different weights of matting.

You will see that in each case there are two values given for the amount of lay-up resin needed for the CSM. The first (lower) figure assumes that a roller will be used in the laminating process so less resin is needed. The second (higher) figure is more suitable if the resin is being applied with a brush only. More resin is needed with this method.

Coverage	Gelcoat required. tissue needs		One layer of surface CSM needs		One layer of 300g/m² CSM needs		One layer of 450g/m² CSM needs		One layer of 600g/m² CSM needs	
	Gelcoat resin	2% hardener	Lay-up resin	2% hardener	Lay-up resin	2% hardener	Lay-up resin	2% hardener	Lay-up resin	2% hardener
0.25m²	150g	3ml	150g	3ml	150-190g	3-4ml	225-280g	5-6ml	300-375g	6-8ml
0.50m²	300g	6ml	300g	6ml	300-375g	6-8ml	450-560g	9-12ml	600-750g	12-15ml
0.75m²	450g	9ml	450g	9ml	450-560g	9-11ml	675-840g	13-17ml	900-1125g	18- 23ml
1.00m²	600g	12ml	600g	12ml	600-750g	12-15ml	900-1125g	18- 23ml	1200-1500g	24-30ml
2.00m²	1200g	24ml	1200g	24ml	1200-1500g	24-30ml	1800-2250g	36-45ml	2400-3000g	48-60ml

Appendix 2
Troubleshooting

Gelcoat problems

Wrinkling

Wrinkles are visible in the gelcoat surface. This is normally due to styrene attack from the laminating resin. The gelcoat may be too thin or not fully cured. Contamination of the gelcoat by cleaning solvents can also cause wrinkling.
- Use a gelcoat layer 0.5mm thick.
- Check the gelcoat for correct curing before laying up the CSM layer.
- Make sure brushes contain no traces of acetone or thinners before use.

Pinholing

Pinholes are visible in the outer gelcoat surface. They are usually due to trapped air bubbles caused by stirring the gelcoat too vigorously when mixing in the pigment or catalyst. Moisture or solvent contamination can also cause pinholing.
- Stir gently but thoroughly when mixing in pigment or catalyst.
- Avoid moisture in the workpiece.
- Make sure brushes contain no traces of acetone or thinners before use.

Lifting away from the mould

The gelcoat can shrink and lift off the mould surface before the CSM is laminated on. This is caused by excess heat or excess catalyst.
- Remove any direct heat sources.
- Reduce the amount of catalyst added to the resin.

Blisters

Raised blisters are visible in the gelcoat surface. This may be due to poor adhesion between the gelcoat and the subsequent layers because the gelcoat has been left for too long before laminating or by poor lamination technique leaving air trapped between the gelcoat and the CSM.
- Laminate onto the gelcoat as soon as it is fully cured or within 24 hours.
- Consolidate CSM layers with a roller and plenty of resin.

Fibre pattern

The pattern of the CSM or woven fabric is visible through the gelcoat. It happens when the gelcoat is too thin or not fully cured before the backing fibres are applied. It can also happen if the panel is removed from the mould before full curing has taken place.
- Use a gelcoat layer 0.5mm thick.
- Check the gelcoat for correct curing before laying up the CSM layer.
- Allow the panel to cure completely before removal from the mould.

Sticking

The component sticks to the mould or plug and will not release. This can be due to incompatible release agents or poor application before use.
- Use release agents designed specifically for GRP use.
- Use release agents designed to be compatible with each other.
- Take care to follow instructions exactly when applying release agents.

Streaking

The gelcoat colour is patchy, streaky or uneven. This is due to the pigment being poorly mixed in the resin or the gelcoat layer being too thin or uneven.

- Stir in the pigment slowly but thoroughly.
- Apply the gelcoat as a consistent 0.5mm thick coating.
- Back up the gelcoat layer with a layer of surface tissue and coloured resin.

Lamination Problems

Bubbles or dry patches

Bubbles or areas of incompletely saturated CSM are visible in the laminate. The causes are lack of resin, using resin which is beginning to set or poor consolidation during lay-up.

- Use the correct quantity of resin for the amount of matting you are using.
- Do not continue to use resin which is beginning to set.
- Take care to thoroughly wet out all the CSM. A roller is preferable to a brush.

Matting lifting away from the laminate

The CSM will not stay attached to the mould or plug even when fully saturated with resin. CSM will not mould to tight curves or sharp edges. It lifts away from a curve or corner leaving air bubbles underneath.

- Butt cut edges of CSM into the corner or edge.
- Thin woven tape may be flexible enough to form the tighter curves.

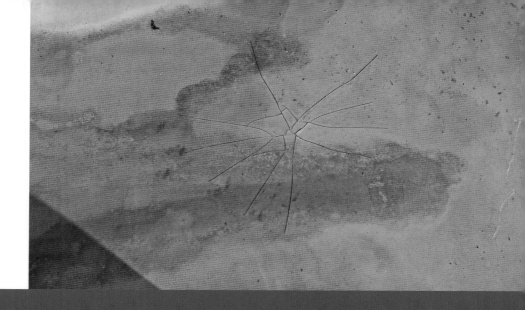

Appendix 3
Glossary of terms

Accelerator: *A chemical, normally pre-mixed with the resin, which reacts with the catalyst to cause the resin to set.*

Barrier Cream: *A cream which is applied to the skin before work begins. It protects the skin from harmful chemicals and also makes it easier to clean when the work is finished.*

Binder: *A material added to the glass fibres to hold them in place in the matting until resin is added. CSM may use emulsion or powder binders.*

Core: *Foam, Coremat, wood, or rolled paper which is skinned with, or placed between layers of CSM to form a sandwich structure.*

Crazing: *Fine cracks which appear in the gelcoat due to impact, bending or stress (see pic above).*

Curing: *The chemical reaction between the catalyst and the resin causing it to change from a liquid to a solid.*

Filler: *A thick paste made by adding an inert powder to liquid resin. It sets solid when catalyst is added. It can be used to fill surface imperfections.*

Fibreglass: *A registered trade mark of Pilkington Glass for their products originally designed for insulation. Like 'Aspirin' and 'Hoover' the term has fallen into generic use.*

Gelcoat: *The thixotropic resin which is added to the mould first and forms the hard outer surface of a GRP moulding.*

GRP: *Glass reinforced plastic. The correct name for what is commonly referred to as 'fibreglass'.*

Lay-up: *The process of adding layers of resin and glassfibre matting to a mould.*

Laminate: *A solid formed from layers of resin and fibreglass.*

Mould: *The former in which you lay-up the final workpiece.*

Plug: *The object from which you make the mould. A plug is an exact copy of the object you are making but it can be made from any material. Only the surface finish is important.*

Ply: *A single layer of matting or cloth soaked in catalysed resin. The more plies you add the thicker the final object will be.*

Release agent: *A material added to the mould to prevent the laminate sticking to it.*

Roving: *Long strands of glass fibres. They can be woven together to produce cloth like materials.*

Thixotropic: *A fluid which lowers its viscosity in response to a shear force. It is a thick liquid until a sideways (painting) force is applied, then it becomes thinner.*

Viscosity: *A measure of the thickness of a liquid. The higher the viscosity of a liquid the less easily it flows.*

Workpiece: *The object that you are in the process of making.*

Appendix 4
Contacts

Adhesives
Intertronics (Araldite structural adhesives)
Unit 17, Station Field Industrial Estate
Banbury Road, Kidlington, Oxfordshire, OX5 1JD
T: +44 (0)1865 842842
E: info@intertronics.co.uk
W: www.intertronics.co.uk/data/ara2015.pdf

Sika Limited (Sikaflex)
Watchmead, Welwyn Garden City, Hertfordshire, AL7 1BQ
T: +44 (0) 1707 394444
E: sales@uk.sika.com
E: technical@uk.sika.com
W: www.sika.co.uk/1-comp_poly_tech-2.pdf

U-POL (Tigerseal)
Totteridge Lane, London, N20 0EY
T: +44 (0)870 8998 220
E: website@u-pol.com
W: www.u-pol.com

Fasteners and Fixings
bigHead Bonding Fasteners Limited
Units 15/16 Elliott Road, West Howe Industrial Estate
Bournemouth, BH11 8LZ
T: +44 (0)1202 574 601
E: info@bigHead.co.uk
W: www.bighead.co.uk

ModelFixings.co.uk (Threaded Inserts)
Nottingham, Highland NG16 1JX
T: +44 (0)115 8548791
E: info@modelfixings.com
W: www.modelfixings.co.uk

Gelcoat Restoration
Farécla Products (UK) Ltd
12, Centrus, Mead Lane, Hertford,
Hertfordshire, SG13 7GX
T: +44 (0)1992 512 680
E: enquiries@farecla.com
W: www.farecla.com/pdfs/Marine%208pp.pdf

GRP Supplies
East Coast Fibreglass Supplies
Unit 2B, Rekendyke Industrial Estate, South Shields,
Tyne and Wear, NE33 5BZ
T: +44 (0)191 4975134
E: sales@ ecfibreglasssupplies.co.uk
W: www.ecfibreglasssupplies.co.uk/store

Safety Equipment
Arco, (Safety Equipment)
PO Box 21, Waverley Street, Hull, HU1 2SJ
W: www.arco.co.uk

Notes

Notes

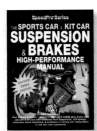

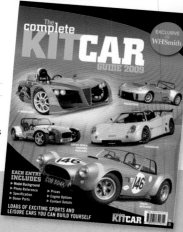